RISK-TAKING

RISK-TAKING

50 Ways to Turn Risks Into Rewards

MARLENE CAROSELLI, Ed.D.
and DAVID HARRIS

SkillPath Publications
Mission, Kansas

Editor: Kelly Scanlon

Cover Design: Rod Hankins

Text Layout: Debi Klein

Library of Congress Catalog Card Number: 95-71715

ISBN: 1-878542-32-X

10   9   8   7   6   5   4   3   2   1   02   03   04   05

Printed in the United States of America

Table of Contents

Part Three: The High Risks—Experiencing Success
Through New Ventures 73

Preface

R isk-Taking: 50 Ways to Turn Risks Into Rewards presents fifty
activities that will increase your desire and ability to take
risks. These activities will encourage you to accept new challenges;
in the process, you will develop your self-esteem.

The key is to challenge yourself to change your behavior, to at least
consider new possibilities. Doing only what is comfortable and
familiar will bring only comfortable and familiar outcomes. If you
are truly interested in being better than you are, if you wish to
expand your boundaries, if you seek to move beyond existing
mundane definitions and discover new depths to your essence, you
will discover in this book what you need to define yourself in a
new light.

The fifty activities progress logically from easy to difficult, calling
for increased resources and resourcefulness as you proceed from
the low- to the high-risk stage. These fifty activities will energize
you. They are not of the fear-producing variety—adrenaline-
pumping, perhaps, but not fear-producing. They do not require all-
or-nothing-at-all gambles. Don't feel as if you must do every single
activity; do not feel you are being urged to move in a lock-step
fashion from #1 to #50, increasing in neat increments the degree of

risk associated with each. Be flexible; do what feels right for you, given your unique circumstances. Only you know when the potential loss is more than you can comfortably bear. When you can and where you can, modify the activity to suit your needs. We do encourage you to do as many of the activities and practices as you can. When you have completed the book, you will have, hopefully, gained the confidence you need to plan your own risk-taking encounters. Part Four contains planning sheets that will help you organize these additional risk-taking endeavors.

Although you don't need to move sequentially through the book, we do recommend that you proceed from the first section to the last section over a period of weeks or months. Ask your co-workers, friends, and family members to give you feedback too. One of the best ways to prove to yourself that you can succeed in your exciting new plans is to have others affirm the changes you are making. Ask for support, but don't depend on it.

This book offers no guarantees. We can't promise that if you faithfully do the activities and practices, you will be transformed into a risk-taker who will always realize a greater return on investments than what the investment cost at the outset.

But we can guarantee that doing these exercises will help you learn more about yourself. And as the ancient Greeks observed, "The unexamined life is not worth living." Armed with expanded self-knowledge, you will be more willing to explore ways to add greater value to your life. You will avoid investments that constitute more than you can afford to lose. Although many of the activities focus on career improvement, particularly in the high-risk section, your increased self-confidence will inevitably spill over to pursuits and relationships beyond the workplace.

No two people will learn from this book in the same way. No two individuals will have identical results. No two people can possibly enjoy the same outcomes. But of this you can be sure: there *will be* outcomes—both tangible and intangible—that you will realize from making this investment in yourself.

The more you do, the more you will profit. Yes, it will be necessary for you to face some fears, to spend some time, to shift some paradigms. But such newness is what makes life worth living. Such newness is necessary if we as individuals and as corporations are to survive and ultimately thrive. The question is not "Should I take a risk?" but rather "What risk should I take?"

The Japanese word *kaizen* means the small successes, the daily conversion of modest opportunities into large-impact improvements in our ways of thinking, behaving, living. Ultimately, the small successes lead to the big breakthroughs. This conversion is, in fact, the purpose behind this book: the acquisition of small successes derived from well-planned, well-executed risks, so that the big breakthroughs—the deserved rewards associated with your hard work—can materialize.

Welcome to the world of risk-takers. The inhabitants of that world exemplify the words of Danish philosopher Soren Kierkegaard: "To dare is to lose one's footing momentarily. To not dare is to lose oneself." We encourage you to take risks. In the process you will find yourself and the best that is in you.

PART ONE

Turning Risks Into Rewards

DEFINING RISK

What is a risk? Quite simply, it is an investment in time, money, or people that may or may not pay off. We all hope, of course, that our investments will pay off, returning to us more than we put in.

Whether the risk involves money, health, career, time, romance, or family, everyone takes risks all day long. Most of these risks are negligible, their consequences of such little importance that we barely consider them risks.

When consequences are of greater importance, however, we are sometimes tempted to consider the situation as being caused by accident or by a force of nature—something that we had no control over. In truth, these situations often begin with our conscious decision to do one thing rather than another.

Californians who experience earthquakes, for example, have knowingly decided to live in that state, believing that the richness it provides in terms of climate or scenery or opportunities outweighs the potential negative consequences of an earthquake. Purchasing insurance is one way people deal with the negative results of the decision to live in places prone to natural disasters. By buying insurance, they hedge their bets against results that may or may not occur. They pay high annual premiums as a cautionary move against what may lie in store. In doing so, they are not reducing the risk—for there are some things people really have no control over—they are merely reducing the potential *cost* of misfortune.

For many people, the word "risk" has a negative connotation. It suggests actions pursued with wild abandon, decisions made carelessly or capriciously. But the most successful individuals do not refrain from risk-taking. They refrain from taking *foolish* risks. They weigh the pros and cons and explore alternatives. Then they make their decision and prepare themselves in the best way possible for the consequences that may occur if their decision proves not to be worth the risk. This is the way the word *risk* is used in this book: as a deliberate, thoughtfully considered series of actions, with an outcome that is believed to yield more than the initial investment of resources.

The real risk in the activities in this book is the risk of change. In fact, some of the activities may not seem like risks at all. They may seem like good, general practices for self-development. But consider this: Any change from your current activities is a risk. You risk being uncomfortable. You risk the uncertainty that change brings. You risk the stability you are accustomed to. But when you get right down to it, these are the real risks with anything different that you try.

No matter what it is you are investing in, there will be some element of the unknown, some danger that things will not go as planned. Experimenting with your potential will mean change. But change is the operative word for the future. The world will not stand still, no matter how much you might wish for constancy.

The status does not remain quo for very long in this day and age. The wise risk-takers—whether they are working on quality-improvement teams to improve processes or whether they are creating new designs for the work flow—are willing to push against the firmly entrenched fences of traditional thought and modes of behavior.

When you take a risk, you are putting something in jeopardy in order to receive a bigger payoff later. When you stand up to make a presentation, for example, you are making an investment in your own self-confidence, self-growth, and professional visibility. The risk aspect comes in when you realize the speech might not go over well. If that happens, then instead of promoting your career, you might do it damage. Instead of developing your self-confidence, a poorly received presentation may do just the opposite: it may cause you to retreat into a shell that you never emerge from.

But like the turtle who will never advance unless he sticks his head out of his shell, you must move out of your comfort zones if you expect to be better than you are. Not all risks will have a successful conclusion; not all of your "investments" in time or money or people will yield results greater than your original outlay. But you can calculate in order to increase the likelihood that the risk will be well-founded. And you can plan in order to minimize the losses that might occur should the risk fall into the debit rather than the credit column of your life-ledger. Even when you fail, you still profit, for you learn something that will make the next occurrence less "risky." Failure can also be a motivating force. When you know you can do better (and your earlier successes will have proven to you that you can), then a temporary setback becomes a learning experience, not a lifelong destiny.

And you will find that when you do succeed, your investment pays off handsomely. The speech that evokes loud applause enhances your stature, increases your faith in your own competence, and motivates you to continue pursuing greater challenges. You get back more than you invested, which is exactly what you hoped would happen.

Risk-taking involves trust—trust in yourself above all else. Only you know how much effort you are willing to exert. Only you know the circumstances surrounding the risk situation. Only you know the consequences of an investment that doesn't pay off. And so, only you can know how much to risk and when to risk it.

If you have confidence that the risk you are contemplating is the wisest possible course of action, and if you have prepared for implementing the risk itself, you should be able to improve your present situation and enhance future situations as well.

SELF-GROWTH

By completing the activities in this book, you will be exerting greater control over the circumstances of your life, especially those of your work life. Thus, you will lessen the draining effect of stress. And when you are energized by your own successes, you will want to try even more. It is a delicious cycle, not a vicious one. The cycle of success begets even greater success.

If you are brave enough to learn more about yourself by completing these activities, if you are willing to engage in self-assessment to discover what needs to be done, what paths need to be followed, then you are making a statement. That statement is, "I am willing to explore ways to improve who I am so I can improve the contribution I can make to others and to the organizations I belong to."

To do so, of course, you must go beyond traditional ways of thinking, of acting, of communicating. You must enhance your self-talk—in some situations, you will be the only person who believes you can really carry out the change you are proposing. To optimize your natural talents, to fulfill your professional destiny, to "grow" yourself, you will need to expect:

- Change.

- Conflict.

- Investment of your resources.

The more quickly you learn to be comfortable with change—which you simply cannot prevent—the more easily you will be able to take risks. The more willing you are to deal with conflict via appropriate win-win strategies, the more likely you are to benefit from your risk endeavors. The more willing you are to make those investments of time or attitude or money, the more firm will be your desire to succeed with your risk initiatives.

You must be committed, though, to overcoming inertia. You must be willing to think some new thoughts, to add another facet to your personality, another skill to your professional repertoire. You must be willing to anticipate that the risk won't prove worthy of your investment. The successful risk-taker considers these questions and others before undertaking any new projects. He or she considers consequences before reaching the stage of needing to.

Turn now to Part Two of this book, where you will learn to build your willingness and ability to take risks by working through twenty-five low-risk activities. Here you are invited to enter the world of risk-takers, an exciting center of self-actualization, self-esteem, and self-empowerment.

The Low Risks— Building Your Willingness to Take Risks

The twenty-five risk-taking activities in this part of the book are devoted to low risks. They require either minimal or no financial cost. These risk activities will give you relatively positive feedback as well as safe, sure, and dependable results—results that you will feel almost immediately.

Yes, these activities do require some action on your part. Some will require you to concentrate on your actions more than others, but each activity is, in fact, low-risk.

Don't worry if you are not able to conjure up the nerve to do some of the activities. You may be afraid that people will think you are crazy if you speak to or smile at them for no reason, for example.

Or you may fear that people won't like you if you take action to correct problems or begin to act more confidently. Again, don't worry. Concentrate on doing the activities you are comfortable with. By the end of this low-risk section of the book, particularly after you've had some success with activities you are most comfortable with, you should be able to go back to the activities that gave you difficulty (if there were any).

The real "risk" with the activities in this section is in taking the action. It is struggling to overcome your inner fear. To reduce your fear, many of the activities contain exercises, or practices, to get you started. Read and understand each activity before attempting it. At first, when an activity has an associated practice, follow the practice. It will help you to get started with carrying out the activity. If you feel comfortable with the practice, look for different situations where you can apply it. If you wish, modify the practices to fit your personal style. Keep the spirit of the activity in mind and try to adhere to it. For some activities, there are no practices. In these cases, the way to carry out the activity is self-evident, so "have at it."

As you work through the activities, keep in mind that sometimes it's better to proceed without even thinking about what you are going to do. Thinking about what action to take can become a "blocker" (something that gets in the way of your taking action). Blockers produce anxiety, which may cause you to talk yourself out of doing something. The practices provide a glimpse of the actions that are necessary to carry out the activity and to reduce the anxiety you may feel about trying.

A large part of the time that it takes to do anything is spent "getting ready to": "I'm getting ready to start my work," "I'm getting ready to write the report," "I'm getting ready to fix the faucet." Once we near a deadline or are pushed, we just get up and do the task. Then we wonder why we waited so long. The practices encourage you to eliminate the "getting-ready-to" time and "have at" the activities.

There are several ways to approach the activities. You don't necessarily need to do them in the sequence presented here. It is also possible to do more than one activity at a time. You may be able to do some of the activities quickly; others will take an extended period of time. The schedule is yours to develop. You will have to decide which activities to do, when to do them, and how long you feel you will need to master each one. Just keep in mind that building your willingness to take risks is not something that is accomplished overnight.

Just smile.

Purpose: To break the ice with the people you interact with each day.

How do you feel when you see someone who is *not* smiling? Do you think that person is a grouch? How do you react inside when others don't smile? How do you think people silently react to you when *you* don't smile? Even though you may be smiling inside, thinking good thoughts, and wishing the world well, it may not be perceptible to others.

Now, stop and think about how you feel when you see someone who *is* smiling. Isn't it pleasant? Even when it seems that the other person is "too happy," doesn't it just feel good to be around a smiling person?

We seldom practice smiling. Smiling doesn't cost a thing, but the payback can be phenomenal. If you smile at someone, that person will usually smile back, particularly if you couple your smile with a hello. Just that one small exchange can brighten the day for you and for the person you greeted. Opening the door to a new friendship can unleash a new world of opportunity. So, try this: Smile at people you are not used to greeting. (You probably already smile at your friends, relatives, and colleagues—but if you don't, start now.)

Okay, some people may think you are weird if you go around smiling at strangers. So what!! More times than not, people will think you're just being friendly, and that's exactly what you are, isn't it? You're just opening up and letting others see how you are feeling on the inside.

And even if you aren't smiling on the inside, smile anyway. You'll be surprised at how soon you'll begin to feel that way. A smile is like your own individual sunshine. It's a gift to those you see. So, follow the lead of the song: Get up each morning and "put on a happy face."

You may feel that going around smiling when it's not heartfelt is phony and artificial. You may even find it uncomfortable and embarrassing. That's okay. Smile anyway. Follow through with the practice for this activity and evaluate the outcome. Decide whether the results you receive aren't well worth the smiles.

You may want to start the practice on an active day. For example, if you interact with more people during the week, then you may want to start on a week day. If you are most active on the weekend, then that's the time to start.

Try the following 30-day experiment.

Days 1-5: For the first five days, count the number of times you meet, greet, or just walk by people. You don't have to make any changes. Just be aware of your behavior. If you like, record your actions on a sheet of paper or in a journal. Did you smile when you encountered others?

Days 6-10: Be sure to smile at those you come in direct contact with. These are people you speak to or interact with anyway—family members, friends, and colleagues.

Days 11-20: Make a point to smile at most folks. These are people you may see often but don't interact with.

Days 21-30: Make a point to smile at everyone!!!

Day 30: Evaluate.

How did it all work out? Did smiling open any doors for you? Create any new opportunities? Pave the way for a new friendship to develop?

_____

_____

_____

_____

_____

_____

_____

_____

_____

_____

#2

Keep a diary or journal.
Purpose: To provide you with an accurate record of your activities so you can evaluate how you use your time. This history will also serve as a measure of your growth and development.

W hat did you do on this day last year? Or on this day a month ago? Or on this day last week? Of course, it's relatively easy to remember important events that have happened recently in your life, but like most people, you may have difficulty pinpointing how you spend your time in general each day.

Recording important events, interactions, thoughts, and the reasons why you did or didn't take an action can be useful for tracing your growth and development. Too often, people view their past through rose-colored glasses, allowing their current situations to distort the way things really were. By keeping a journal, you can compile an accurate history of your life, which you can use as a frame of reference to compare your future experiences against.

There are several ways to keep a journal. You can purchase a diary or a book of blank pages. You can jot notes in your day planner or date book. Many planners provide journal space. Or, you can enter notes in a loose-leaf notebook. You may even want to enter your thoughts on a computer. Whichever method you choose, use it consistently.

Keep your diary or journal for an entire year. Stick to it. Resist the temptation to put off making your entries. Be sure to make well-rounded notes that capture what is going on in both your personal life and your career.

Bear in mind that you are not keeping a planning journal or a record of goal achievement. Rather you are recording each day's activities and then reflecting on them.

At the beginning or end of each day, spend ten to fifteen minutes assessing how you used your time for the period of your last entry. Also analyze how you used your money and other resources. Did you build any new relationships? How did you handle any nonroutine occurrences?

#3

Be positive.

Purpose: To develop the capacity to recognize and celebrate the many good things in life rather than to waste energy focusing on the negative.

Work to see the positive side of life's events. Why bother? Because when your outlook on life is positive, even those areas of your life that are problematic tend to seem less difficult and more manageable.

Try the following exercise.

List several things that have happened to you today. Then rate them in terms of how they affect you either positively or negatively.

	Negative				Positive

1. _____   1------2------3------4------5

2. _____   1------2------3------4------5

3. _____   1------2------3------4------5

4. _____   1------2------3------4------5

5. _____   1------2------3------4------5

Using the same scale of 1 to 5, rate how you feel today.

1------2------3------4------5

Now consider the most positive thing that has happened to you—ever. Think about that experience for a few minutes. What was going on during this positive experience? Who was a part of it? What were the surroundings? What were you feeling? What did things smell like? Visualize all of these things in your mind. Close your eyes for a few minutes and just think about that experience. Try to relive it.

Now, how do you feel? Rate yourself again on the five-point scale.

1------2------3------4------5

Look at the five items that you listed and rated in the first part of this exercise. How do you feel about those events now? Rate them again, noticing whether there has been any change since you rated them the first time. Chances are, there is. When you put yourself in a positive frame of mind, you tend to view things positively. On the other hand, when you constantly dwell on the negative, you'll find that fewer of life's events go your way. You'll also find that you've expended a lot of time and energy on things you can't change. Your resulting anger and frustration will sap you of the energy you need to move forward and succeed, both in your career and in your personal affairs.

Practice

You *can* control your outlook. For the next 21 days, try to look for the positive side of every situation. State what is positive out loud to yourself. When anyone asks you how you are doing, answer that you are doing great—whether you are or not.

Take time each day to do a "positiveness" check, to ask yourself how you are doing on the five-point scale. You may be surprised to see so many "5s" by the end of the 21-day period.

	Positive Occurrence	Positiveness Check
Day 1		1----2----3----4----5
Day 2		1----2----3----4----5
Day 3		1----2----3----4----5
Day 4		1----2----3----4----5
Day 5		1----2----3----4----5
Day 6		1----2----3----4----5
Day 7		1----2----3----4----5
Day 8		1----2----3----4----5
Day 9		1----2----3----4----5
Day 10		1----2----3----4----5
Day 11		1----2----3----4----5
Day 12		1----2----3----4----5
Day 13		1----2----3----4----5
Day 14		1----2----3----4----5
Day 15		1----2----3----4----5
Day 16		1----2----3----4----5
Day 17		1----2----3----4----5
Day 18		1----2----3----4----5
Day 19		1----2----3----4----5
Day 20		1----2----3----4----5
Day 21		1----2----3----4----5

#4

Do something step by step.

Purpose: To develop the ability to organize complex and mind-boggling tasks into manageable and achievable steps.

A re problems and events sometimes so large that they over-whelm you? Do you sometimes just give up and let them? Learn to keep your projects or tasks manageable by completing them *step by step*. Or, if you're already in the midst of a project that is quickly becoming overwhelming, take steps now to regain control.

There are two things you must do to regain or keep control. First, you must keep the big picture in mind. Second, you must dissect the problem (or event) into manageable parts and then do them step by step.

Both of these steps are important. Without the "big picture," you can easily become engrossed in minor, mundane details. But to concentrate only on the "big picture" can result in feeling over-whelmed and losing sight of the important details necessary to accomplish the total task. So, both the big picture and the minor details work hand in hand for a balance that enables you to achieve and maintain your stability.

To regain control of a task, you must first define the problem or problems. Write them in clear, simple, complete, narrative sentences. Then write out any deadlines associated with the task. It would also be wise to write down any other important dates and deadlines you may have, even if they aren't associated with this particular task. Also write down the resources you have available to perform the task—people, finances, time, equipment, and so forth. Ask yourself whether you have all you need to be successful. If not, try to negotiate the resources that you will need.

Next, list every step necessary for accomplishing the task. At first, don't try to put these in any order. Just write them all down. This process is called *brainstorming*. After brainstorming by yourself, you may want to involve others who are involved in the task. Brainstorming, both separately and as a group, offers two different sets of dynamics, two different perspectives. If you are the only one involved in the task, you may want to engage the support of a friend or colleague just for a different perspective.

Once you have listed all the steps, sort them in reverse chronological order from their anticipated completion date. Allocate and commit the resources necessary for each step. Then assign a date each step must be completed by as well as a person who will be responsible for completing it. Then, step by step, just perform the task.

"Check in" with yourself periodically to ensure that you are on track. If your schedule needs adjusting, you can do so with enough time to still meet your deadlines. This should help you to keep the "big picture" in perspective.

If you carefully think out and execute each step and if you check in periodically and readjust as necessary, you will be able to complete the task step by step.

Above all, avoid doing a task all at once. Remember: Dissect "big" problems into smaller, more manageable parts. Someone once said that "we should eat the mastodon one bit at a time."

#5

Set your goals.

Purpose: To establish a systematic way to set and evaluate goals and then to complete them.

Think about the following questions. Then jot down your reactions on the lines provided.

What will you be doing this time next year?

_____

_____

_____

What will you be doing five years from now, or in twenty years?

_____

_____

_____

Are you having difficulty with this exercise? Why?

_____

_____

_____

_____

Did you answer that you don't know what's going to happen in the future? Was part of your answer that "it all depends on what happens" or that you *"hope* to be doing something like . . . ?"

Often, people think of their future in terms of the *opportunities* it holds, and they often perceive those opportunities as being in the hands of someone or something else. Believing that their destinies are not in their hands, they are leery of setting goals. Is that what has happened to you?

Do you hesitate to consider your goals because you are unable to forecast the future? Do you believe that setting and achieving your goals depends on other people's actions? Do you view goal-setting as presupposing that you know what your future opportunities will be? How often have you heard people say: "I can't set goals. I don't know what things will be like tomorrow." Are you one of these people?

It is true that no one can *totally* control his or her future. Consequently, the realization of your goals is not entirely in your hands. But you do have a great deal of influence over your future.

It is important to set realistic and achievable goals and to write them down. Start with a long-term goal and then set several small goals that will help you achieve your larger one. (See Activity #4.)

Communicate these goals to others. If you have questions about how to achieve a particular goal, get help.

Don't worry about your future and whether it unfolds as you imagine it will. As you develop as a person, things will invariably change. You will often outgrow your plan. It will need updating, revamping, and rewriting. Plan to review your goals and to continually develop your goal setting.

Long-range goals are those that you set for more than five years from now. They may be lifelong goals. As you set your long-range goals, consider what you really want out of life. Also, remember that long-range goals influence intermediate- and short-range goals.

Intermediate-range goals are those you plan to accomplish in the next five years. These goals are actually much more concrete long-range goals. They are better conceived, and you have much greater control over them. You can "see" and "feel" five-year goals; therefore, they seem "doable." Within a five-year time period, you can attend college and earn a degree. You can plan to marry and have children. It is said that in America, anyone can change his or her life in just four years, so think what you are capable of doing in five years.

Although you will develop your five-year plan with your long-range plan in mind, it is your five-year plan that will give you a goal that you can really "sink your teeth into," especially as you break it down into goals for the next twelve months.

Goals that you set for the next twelve months are your *short-range goals*. These are the goals you work toward from day to day. They are built around your five-year goals, but they are broken down into smaller, much more manageable, everyday tasks. Although the goals you set for the next twelve months are the ones you will be able to influence the most, you may work at these goals for only a short time and then get busy with other things. Frequently, reviewing your goals may take a back seat to your other business. Your goals may get shoved aside. But, reviewing your goals is important. Reviewing them helps you to stay on track.

In short, consider what you want out of life and use that as a starting point for setting long-term goals. Then decide what is required of you in the next five years to achieve them. Finally, establish goals for the next twelve months to help you reach your five-year goals.

Remember: 1. Communicate your goals to others.

2. Get help in reaching your goals.

3. Review your goals.

Get to know people.

Purpose: To take full advantage of your daily opportunities to develop and expand your contacts into friendships.

H ow often do you walk right by people without knowing who they are? You may see these people; sometimes, you may even talk with them and know their names, *but do you know them?*

As part of this activity, you will get to know people. This is not to suggest that you walk up to perfect strangers, introduce yourself, and try to get to know them better. It is not even to suggest that you walk up to acquaintances and colleagues and pepper them with questions about their business and private lives.

Simply look at the people around you. Of the people you interact with each day, how much do you really know about them?

In a very short period of time, you'd be surprised at how much you can learn about people. When people believe that you are genuinely interested in them, they will be more interested in you.

How will getting to know people help you in your life? You never know. You may be able to help each other as you move onward and upward to greater success. It certainly helps to have someone support your efforts, whether it is in your career or in your personal life. You may have mutual interests such as hobbies that have nothing to do with career advancement. Or, you may gain inner satisfaction from helping someone else without expecting or receiving anything in return.

Practice

Knowing Folks Assessment

List ten people you come in contact with regularly.

1. _____   6. _____
2. _____   7. _____
3. _____   8. _____
4. _____   9. _____
5. _____   10. _____

For each person you listed, can you answer the following questions? In each column, enter "Y" (yes) if you can or "N" (no) if you can't.

	Person #1	Person #2	Person #3	Person #4	Person #5	Person #6	Person #7	Person #8	Person #9	Person #10
Is the person married?										
Does the person have children? If so, how old are they?										
How is the person employed?										
What are the person's job responsibilities?										
What are the person's life aspirations?										
Does this person have any hobbies?										
What skills does this person have that aren't work-related?										
What does this person do for entertainment?										

Now, select one of the people on your list. Over the next month, talk with that person. See whether you can get the information you need to change your "no" answers to "yes."

#7

Increase and practice your repertoire of responses.

Purpose: To prepare yourself for difficult, anxiety-producing situations and turn them into opportunities to excel.

H ave you ever been in a disagreeable situation and later thought of several ways you could have or should have handled the situation but didn't? Many people have. Wouldn't it have been better if you had thought out your options before the situation and had them at your disposal then rather than afterwards?

Pre-think, pre-visualize, pre-practice your responses. Doing so will better prepare you for the appropriate response during tense and anxiety-producing situations. Your response will be thoroughly thought out and less reactive.

As a start, think about the difficult situations in your life that need to be addressed. What are some of the ways you may handle or resolve these situations? As you think through your responses, you may even want to ask others for advice on how they have handled similar situations. Remember, however, that what works as a solution for one person may not be such a good solution for someone else. Still, develop several potential responses to the situations you have identified. When and if the situation for which you have prepared arises, you will have to make a judgment call as to which "reaction" is most appropriate for that specific situation.

Practice

Select three situations you have some difficulty handling. Rank them according to their likelihood of occurring in the next month. Some of these may even be recurring situations. Enter the response you can take to the situation in the "Responses" column. Then rehearse each response. Each time you rehearse a response, enter a check mark in the "Rehearsed" column.

Before you rehearse each response, take a moment to think about the situation. Visualize it in your mind. See it and the people involved. What are the questions, comments, and reactions the others involved are likely to have? How will you respond to each of these? Think about the outcome you wish for the situation. Role play the situation, if possible.

You may want to record your responses on an audio tape and play it back to yourself. You can achieve two things by doing so. First, you will be able to tell whether you are responding the way you want to. If you're not, keep at it. Make the necessary modifications. Then practice until you are responding just the way you want to. Second, you can play the tape back to refresh yourself and reinforce the repertoire that you are developing.

The bottom line is this: The better prepared you are, the greater the likelihood you will influence the anticipated situation to yield a positive outcome.

Situation #1 _____

_____

Responses		Rehearsed
A.	_____	☐
B.	_____	☐
C.	_____	☐

Situation #2 _____

_____

Responses		Rehearsed
A.	_____	☐
B.	_____	☐
C.	_____	☐

Situation #3 _____

_____

Responses		Rehearsed
A.	_____	☐
B.	_____	☐
C.	_____	☐

#8

Enhance your self-esteem.

Purpose: To identify and focus on the things you already do well. As you develop your self-esteem, your confidence in your risk-taking ability will increase.

Building your self-esteem is not easy. As important as it is for you to feel good about yourself and confident about what you do, you may feel that there are more things in your life that tear down rather than enhance your self-esteem.

Actually, most people do much more right than they do wrong. This is probably true of you too—more than likely you place a great deal more importance on the things you do wrong than on those you do well. In this activity, you will focus on the things you do well.

Although this exercise may seem a little silly and embarrassing, particularly at the beginning, do it anyway. Just ask yourself this question: "If I can't depend on myself to provide feedback on what I do well, why should I require it and demand it from others?" Further, you know yourself better than any other person does. If your judgment is faulty, then just imagine how faulty the judgment of others may be of you.

Practice

In the "Week 1" column, list ten things that you do well. (There are no limits on the types of things you can list.)

	Week 1	Week 2	Week 3
1.	_____	_____	_____
2.	_____	_____	_____
3.	_____	_____	_____
4.	_____	_____	_____
5.	_____	_____	_____
6.	_____	_____	_____
7.	_____	_____	_____
8.	_____	_____	_____
9.	_____	_____	_____
10.	_____	_____	_____

During the first week, as you are brushing your teeth or washing your face, look yourself in the eye and tell yourself that you have the talents, skills, and abilities you listed. Be sure to remind yourself of them each and every day. As you move through the week, you may want to note the times when you demonstrate those skills and abilities. At the end of the first week, return to the practice and develop a list of ten different skills and abilities. Enter this next set of items in the "Week 2" column. During the second week, read the "Week 2" column to yourself each day.

As the third week approaches, develop a third list of skills and abilities. Again, read those items to yourself each day. Be sure to look yourself in the eye when you read the items.

ACTIVITY

#9

Determine your strengths and weaknesses and then analyze them.

Purpose: To get to know yourself objectively so that you can develop a base from which to plan for systematic improvement.

E veryone has strengths and weaknesses. Analyzing them is perhaps one of the greatest personal risks you will take, for it requires you to take an objective look deep inside yourself. But as difficult as this may be, it is incumbent on you to determine exactly what your strengths and weaknesses are. It is the first step in being able to use your strengths to further your career and personal goals and to turn your weaknesses into strengths. The process is ongoing and lifelong.

There are several approaches you can use for this assessment.

Many tests—interest inventories, skills assessments, aptitude tests, ability assessments—are offered as part of career development programs to assist people in determining their strengths and weaknesses. The interpretation, application, and use of many of these tests require a very skilled and competent professional. Remember, however, that these tests provide only a "snapshot" of *some* of your strengths and weaknesses.

One of the easiest and best ways to determine your strengths is to brainstorm the areas in which you have some experience, knowledge, education, or training. Brainstorming allows you to list these areas without placing a value on your degree of strength in them.

No matter which approach you use for this self-assessment—whether you measure your strengths and weaknesses against yourself, a colleague, a role model, or some abstract ideal—you'll find that you are better in some things than you are in others. This is true of everyone.

Remember as you perform this analysis that you know more about yourself than any test can determine and that these tests are only *aids* to self-understanding.

Use the practice that follows to begin the assessment of your strengths and weaknesses.

Practice

In this practice, list your experiences, knowledge, education, training, hobbies, and other activities. Then go back and rate yourself on how well you do them. Use three gauges in your evaluation. First, rate your ability to perform the task if you were at your peak. Then rate yourself against the best person in the field. Finally, compare yourself to the ideal. (Even the best person in the field may not be the ideal. Salespeople are always breaking old sales records; athletes surpass long-standing marks.) Use complete thoughts as you rate yourself.

The rating standards are as follows:

1 = I have acquired some knowledge or initial information.
2 = I can perform at the very basic level.
3 = I could hold an entry-level position.
4 = I am an expert in the area.
5 = I am the very best by current standards.

For each item that you list, place a number from 1 to 5 in the boxes under each of the three categories.

Any item that you can't rate "very best" could be an item for you to work on. Stated differently, it is an item that you could consider a weakness.

	At Peak	Best Person in the Field	The Ideal
Experience			
1. _____	☐	☐	☐
2. _____	☐	☐	☐
3. _____	☐	☐	☐
4. _____	☐	☐	☐
5. _____	☐	☐	☐
Knowledge			
1. _____	☐	☐	☐
2. _____	☐	☐	☐
3. _____	☐	☐	☐
4. _____	☐	☐	☐
5. _____	☐	☐	☐
Education			
1. _____	☐	☐	☐
2. _____	☐	☐	☐
3. _____	☐	☐	☐
4. _____	☐	☐	☐
5. _____	☐	☐	☐

Training

1. _____ ☐ ☐ ☐

2. _____ ☐ ☐ ☐

3. _____ ☐ ☐ ☐

4. _____ ☐ ☐ ☐

5. _____ ☐ ☐ ☐

Hobbies

1. _____ ☐ ☐ ☐

2. _____ ☐ ☐ ☐

3. _____ ☐ ☐ ☐

4. _____ ☐ ☐ ☐

5. _____ ☐ ☐ ☐

Other Activities

1. _____ ☐ ☐ ☐

2. _____ ☐ ☐ ☐

3. _____ ☐ ☐ ☐

4. _____ ☐ ☐ ☐

5. _____ ☐ ☐ ☐

You could also use this process to assess your weaknesses. List your weaknesses and then rate yourself using the same criteria you used to assess your strengths. Remember, this practice provides only a first look. The answers you find will become the base for a broader analysis.

#10

Find ways to influence your environment.

Purpose: To find the best opportunities for success and satisfaction rather than to concentrate on sources of frustration.

You can try to control other people, circumstances, and events, but the only real control you can exercise is that which others *allow you* to exert over them. On the other hand, the only control others can exercise over you is that which *you allow* them to exercise. Ultimately, you have control only of yourself. And even then you do not have total control. There are some limits.

But if you take control of what you *can* in your life, there will be great opportunity for you to influence your environment. The more you are able to control yourself, the greater your opportunity to influence. Look for opportunities to positively influence your environment whether at work or at home, and do it. The more often you do, the greater your success and satisfaction will be.

Brainstorm for ten minutes about the areas of your life you are able to exercise control over. List them on the lines below. Who is affected by your actions? How are these people influenced? What things and events are influenced by your actions?

_____

_____

_____

_____

_____

_____

_____

_____

_____

_____

Select five items from your brainstorming session and enter them in the first column below. Then answer the questions in each column. Finally, select one of the items and take action. Find a way to use it as an opportunity to positively influence your environment.

What in your life can you control?	Who is affected? How?	What thing or event is affected? How?	Will you take action?
1.			
2.			
3.			
4.			
5.			

#11

Accept responsibility only for what you are responsible for.

Purpose: To clarify for yourself and others the obligations you've accepted and to avoid accepting unwanted obligations by default.

What are you really responsible for? Have you ever been blamed for and then accepted responsibility for something you have little or no control over? Does your supervisor give you assignments without providing the resources and authority to carry out the task? Do others—your children, spouse, friends, relatives, or associates—have undefined expectations of you? Do you have undefined expectations of yourself?

Determine what you are truly responsible for. You can be responsible only for those things you agree to. Think about it. You perform a task, and the outcome flows from there. Well-planned and prudent behavior usually results in a desired outcome, but not always.

The practice for this activity provides you with a method for more clearly assigning and accepting commitments. It helps you to see what others expect of you as well as what you have agreed to do. It can put others on notice as to what you have not accepted responsibility for. This mechanism pulls expectations out of the realm of the abstract and makes things a little more manageable.

Practice

Think of five people who have implied expectations of you. List each of those people in the spaces provided. Then, starting with the person you feel most comfortable with, ask each person to clarify five expectations he or she has of you. Write them down. Insist that these people list the behavioral ways in which you can accomplish their expectations. Select one of the behaviors and write it in the appropriate space. Next, consider what you are prepared to do about those expectations and list your commitment.

Person #1 _____

Expectations/Behaviors
1. _____
2. _____
3. _____
4. _____
5. _____

Selected Behavior _____

Commitment _____

Person #2 _____

Expectations/Behaviors
1. _____
2. _____
3. _____
4. _____
5. _____

Selected Behavior _____

Commitment _____

Person #3 _____

Expectations/Behaviors   1. _____

                                 2. _____

                                 3. _____

                                 4. _____

                                 5. _____

Selected Behavior _____

Commitment _____

Person #4 _____

Expectations/Behaviors   1. _____

                                 2. _____

                                 3. _____

                                 4. _____

                                 5. _____

Selected Behavior _____

Commitment _____

Person #5 _____

Expectations/Behaviors   1. _____

                                 2. _____

                                 3. _____

                                 4. _____

                                 5. _____

Selected Behavior _____

Commitment _____

Manage your own time.

Purpose: To analyze the way you use time and, if necessary, make changes to use it more wisely.

Life is time. We measure all that we do by time. Our yardsticks are our appointments, the hours and days of the week, our age, and so on. It stands to reason, then, that if you do not manage your time, you will *waste* time and, consequently, waste some part of your life. As you can see, it is important to manage your time well.

That is not to say that all of your time should be strictly regimented to perform certain activities. But because all activities take time, they will begin to manage you if you do not manage them.

Whether you realize it or not, you do manage your time in some ways. You allow yourself time to go to school and work. You set aside time for family. Although you may feel that you have little control over these and similar activities, they are still managed events. The question is, Who or what controls your time? Is it you, your supervisor, your spouse or children, your peers? Or are the events themselves in control? Are you on automatic pilot? Do things just happen to you?

It is important to understand that whoever controls your time has that control because you have allowed it. It is also important to note that only you can manage your time best. Only you fully know the extent of your commitments and responsibilities. It is you who feels your anxiety when your commitments exceed your ability to meet them. And it is you who will reap the rewards of managing your time well.

Use the practice that follows to construct a 24-hour-a-day, seven-day-a-week schedule for the next week. Enter all the time you have committed so far, including the time that you sleep, eat, work, and rest. Add any activities and obligations that arise as the week progresses. Also enter the time that you travel to and from your commitments and the time that you don't do anything. At the end of the week, ask yourself: How am I spending my time?

Look for opportunities to consolidate events and activities. For example, if you are learning a new skill, are you able to practice while you are traveling to and from work? Can you listen to language tapes while you exercise, or watch a videotape as you prepare dinner? What activities can you or will you change? Will you reduce the amount of television you watch each week? Or will you reduce the amount of time you spend on something else so that you have more time for watching television? Make adjustments to your schedule. Once you have constructed a workable schedule, stick to it.

Practice

	Sun.	Mon.	Tues.	Wed.	Thurs.	Fri.	Sat.
5:00 a.m.							
6:00 a.m.							
7:00 a.m.							
8:00 a.m.							
9:00 a.m.							
10:00 a.m.							
11:00 a.m.							
12:00 p.m.							
1:00 p.m.							
2:00 p.m.							
3:00 p.m.							
4:00 p.m.							
5:00 p.m.							
6:00 p.m.							
7:00 p.m.							
8:00 p.m.							
9:00 p.m.							
10:00 p.m.							
11:00 p.m.							
12:00 a.m.							
1:00 a.m.							
2:00 a.m.							
3:00 a.m.							
4:00 a.m.							

#13

Take control of your finances.

Purpose: To practice getting the most out of the money you already have.

O ne of the most important things you can do is to manage well the resources that you have, those that you actually possess. The resources that you have are the proverbial "bird in the hand." Yet many people complain about what they don't have and struggle to get more before they utilize the resources they already have. This is not to suggest that you should not strive for greater financial achievement. But getting as much as you can out of what you already have could have the impact of extra income.

Start with a long-term financial plan. (This process is similar to the goal-setting process described in Activity #5.) Then establish intermediate goals and objectives based on your long-term goal. Next, establish short-term objectives. Finally, break down your short-term objectives into monthly objectives and adhere to them.

Practice

What is the financial position you wish to be in twenty years from now? Be specific. Take a few moments to relax in a comfortable place and visualize yourself in twenty years. What kind of life would you like to be leading then? What kind of conditions do you envision for your family members? What kind of house would you like to be living in? Now, write a paragraph describing that financial condition.

_____

_____

_____

_____

_____

_____

_____

_____

What are the ten most important things you must do in the next five years to meet the financial vision you just described?

1. _____   6. _____

2. _____   7. _____

3. _____   8. _____

4. _____   9. _____

5. _____   10. _____

What do you have to do in the next twelve months to support those objectives? Plan to accomplish these objectives by setting a twelve-month financial goal. Write a budget to meet those goals. Although the budget will be for only twelve months, keep your five-year financial agenda in mind. Adhere to it and you will improve your financial situation.

Say "no"! And really mean it!

Purpose: To take control of yourself so that you don't let others force you into doing things you don't want to do.

If we expect our children to say "no," then why can't we?

Your capacity to do work is limited. That's because work takes time, and time is a limited resource. Regardless of how much you increase your productivity by using technology or by becoming more efficient, there is only so much, even at maximum capacity, that you can do. Consequently, you must select some tasks to accomplish and others that you will leave alone; that is, sometimes you will have to say "no."

Believe it or not, you do actually say "no" many times a day. You say the biggest and most powerful "no" with your behavior. If you pass someone on the street who asks you for spare change and you continue to walk without answering, you have said "no" without actually uttering the word. Or consider this. If you agree to do something (that is, you say "yes"), but fail to follow through with your commitment, is that not saying "no"?

As you interact with others each day, you are constantly accepting commitments. Some of these commitments are clearly articulated. You simply agree to do something for someone. But many of these commitments aren't quite so clear. These are tasks that are thrust on you or that you become responsible for as a result of expectations and assumptions, even if you didn't agree to them. They just sort of became yours. If you do not want these commitments, you must learn to say "no" to them. Quit "letting" them become your responsibility.

The first step in saying "no" is determining your capacity for work. That way you'll know how much you can take on. (Some of the previous activities—9, 11, and 12—will help you with this.) Then you must decide what is the most important use of your time.

Next, establish a list of items or tasks that are most important for you to accomplish, that are consistent with your goals and values. Call it your "Important To Do" list. Say "no" to anyone and everyone who wants you to do anything that isn't on your "Important To Do" list. If your supervisor, colleagues, significant other, children, or friends require more of you than you have the capacity to deliver, you will have to tell them "no." You can say it kindly, but firmly. Decide when you mean "no" and say it. Say it verbally and say it in your behavior.

If you mean "no," you must say so, above all else, to yourself. Again, you and only you truly understand your capacity. Besides, if you exceed your capacity, you will, in fact, be saying "no" anyway by not keeping your commitment. Saying "no" in this way often leads to negative consequences. Tell yourself "no" when you feel yourself ready to accept more than you can handle.

We generally think of a "no" response as being negative. But consider this view: If you have analyzed your capacity to accomplish things and have decided what is important, your "no" is not negative. It is allowing you the time, energy, and resources to accomplish what is really important to you and helping you to filter out the negatives that get in the way of your goals. Thus, your "no" is really a positive.

ACTIVITY

#15

Don't put others down.

Purpose: To develop the habit of seeing good in others.

Don't put others down. You may say that you don't put others down. Think about that. Do you talk about the weaknesses of others? Do you tell them what those weaknesses are? Do you talk about their weaknesses to other people? If so, why do you do that? Do you find that you get caught up with the group and go along with the negative things that others say so they won't look down on you?

Perhaps now you are backpedaling a bit and saying that all you are doing is telling people the truth—that the people you are making these comments about deserve them. Do they really?

Do these people do anything positive? How many positive comments do you make about them?

If you are like many people, much of what you point out about others is negative. You can do better. Look for the good that people do, even if you're in a situation where you risk the backlash of others because of your views. Instead of assuming that people are bad, assume that they are good. More often than not, you will find that people are indeed good. Further, focusing on what is good in others will give you greater opportunity to help them improve because your positive comments will bolster their self-confidence.

Practice

List the names of five people you are in contact with regularly—relatives, friends, acquaintances, perhaps someone at work. Select one of these as a focus person. Write a paragraph describing what you think or how you feel about the person you selected. Put that paragraph in an envelope and seal it. Write the date on the envelope.

For the next 21 days, observe this person. At the end of each day, regardless of the kind of interaction you had with the person, list at least one *good* thing you observed.

Person _____

Observation

Day 1 _____

_____

Day 2 _____

_____

Day 3 _____

_____

Day 4 _____

_____

Day 5 _____

_____

Day 6 _____

_____

Day 7 _____

_____

Day 8 _____

Day 9 _____

Day 10 _____

Day 11 _____

Day 12 _____

Day 13 _____

Day 14 _____

Day 15 _____

Day 16 _____

Day 17 _____

Day 18 _____

Day 19 _____

Day 20 _____

Day 21 _____

At the conclusion of the exercise, write a paragraph describing what you now think of the person. Then open the envelope and read your first paragraph. Think back to when you wrote that first paragraph. Has anything changed? Do you feel the same about that person as you did three weeks ago?

#16

Benchmark against the best.

Purpose: To identify the best in yourself and in others and to strive for it.

I f you measure yourself against those who are the best in your field, you will be holding yourself up to high standards. Your expectations of what you can achieve will grow as you accomplish more and more.

But finding the best in your field may take some resources. Who is the best? Where are they?

Start by looking at your major roles or at areas that interest you. Then identify the local, regional, national, and even international organizations in those areas. Join these organizations and get involved in the professional activities. You will meet people and become involved in activities that can help you stay up to date on the changes that are taking place. The roles you identify may be either career-related or something that you spend your leisure time doing.

Write each of the areas you identify on the lines on the next page. Then, enter the name, address, telephone number, and the name of the contact for the local, regional, national, or international organization in the spaces provided. A good place to start gathering this information is the telephone book. Your local or college library (particularly community college library) may be of some help too.

Write and call each of these organizations. Ask for information about the organization and determine how it can help you. At a minimum, each organization should be able to help you understand what others in your field are doing and offer opportunities for sharing new ideas.

Don't be surprised if it is sometimes easier to establish contact with the national organizations before you are able to locate the local and regional ones. Even so, it's worthwhile to communicate with each organization at each level.

Practice

	Local	Regional	National	International
AREA				
Organization's Name				
Address				
Phone Number				
Point of Contact				
AREA				
Organization's Name				
Address				
Phone Number				
Point of Contact				

AREA

Organization's Name

Address

Phone Number

Point of Contact

AREA

Organization's Name

Address

Phone Number

Point of Contact

AREA

Organization's Name

Address

Phone Number

Point of Contact

AREA

Organization's Name

Address

Phone Number

Point of Contact

#17

Learn something new—develop a new skill.

Purpose: To invest in yourself.

W hat have you always wanted to do but have never had (or never taken) the time to do? Most people have a mental list of "If I would have . . ., could have . . ., should haves . . ."

- "If I would have continued my education…"
- "I could have been a doctor."
- "I should have saved more of my money."

Your list can easily grow very long. But don't let it get to that point. Start doing something about the items on your mental list. Use it as a starting point for doing or learning something new. Take the time to draft your list—to commit it to paper. What is it that you wish you had done? What is it that you wish you could do? Don't limit your thinking. Include things you wish you'd done as a child or things you should have done as recently as last week. You could learn something new to improve your own work productivity or something that you can teach to others, such as your children.

In many cases, learning something new takes no more than a few hours a week. Find ways to work some of the learning into your

52   *Risk-Taking*

daily routine. For example, if you want to learn a foreign language, purchase a good phrase book and set a goal to learn five to ten phrases a day. Or purchase language tapes that you can listen to on the way to and from work. Don't overlook the courses offered by your community college.

Practice

Brainstorm the things that you wish you could do. Don't limit your ideas. Then select something from the list and *do* it.

1. _____
2. _____
3. _____
4. _____
5. _____
6. _____
7. _____
8. _____
9. _____
10. _____
11. _____
12. _____
13. _____
14. _____
15. _____
16. _____
17. _____
18. _____
19. _____

#18

Analyze and determine the strengths and weaknesses of an organization.

Purpose: To identify opportunities for improvement and to become more valuable to the organizations you belong to.

Consider all the organizations you are a member of. Often, the only organizations people think of are the ones they are associated with through work. However, community organizations, your family, your religious institutions, and your social "circle" are all organizations too.

The strengths and weaknesses of these organizations have a tremendous impact on your ability to perform and to accomplish your goals—just as your own strengths and weaknesses do. However, identifying an organization's strengths and weaknesses is not always easy. Why? Because an organization is the outcome of a number of personalities interacting in different ways. As difficult as it is for you as an individual to analyze your strengths and weaknesses, the task is compounded when you have to consider all the individual and group interactions that take place in an organization. In spite of the difficulty, assessing the organization's strengths and weaknesses will provide you with insight into the organization and will give you an opportunity to assist the organization, making you a more valuable employee or member.

Practice

Begin the organizational assessment by answering some basic questions. What does the organization do? Why? Where does it carry out these activities? What resources are needed? Write your answers to these questions below. Use complete thoughts. Add more questions if you'd like.

What does your organization do?

1. _____
2. _____
3. _____
4. _____
5. _____
6. _____
7. _____

Why?

1. _____
2. _____
3. _____
4. _____
5. _____
6. _____
7. _____

Where does it carry out these activities?

1. _____
2. _____
3. _____
4. _____
5. _____
6. _____
7. _____

What resources are needed?

1. _____
2. _____
3. _____
4. _____
5. _____
6. _____
7. _____

Additional questions:

1. _____
2. _____
3. _____
4. _____
5. _____
6. _____
7. _____

#19

Identify and overcome "blockers."

Purpose: To aggressively identify and overcome the obstacles that keep you from achieving your goals.

A "blocker" is anything that prevents you from doing something that you need or want to do. It could be a circumstance or a lack of resources. It could be that you don't have all the skills that you need to do a particular job or activity. Or you could fear failure, or even success.

The types of blockers are endless. But often you may not even be aware of what your blockers are. When that is the case, how can you compensate for them and overcome them? You can't. You must identify your blockers before you can overcome them.

Take a few minutes to think about a time when you were unable to accomplish a goal. What kept you from that goal? What were your blockers?

Practice

To help you identify and overcome your blockers, focus on three events in your life when you did not accomplish your goals. Use the questions below to identify the blockers in each event and then to brainstorm ways to overcome them.

Event 1

    A. Identify the event in four to ten words.

    _____

    _____

    B. Describe the circumstances in one paragraph.

    _____

    _____

    _____

    _____

    C. What kept you from accomplishing your task or delayed your progress?

    _____

    _____

    _____

    D. What could you have done to avoid the blocker(s)? What were your options for correcting the blocker(s)?

    _____

    _____

    _____

    E. Are you likely to encounter this type of blocker again?

    _____

    _____

    If so, what are you going to do about it?

    _____

    _____

Event 2

    A. Identify the event in four to ten words.

_____

_____

_____

    B. Describe the circumstances in one paragraph.

_____

_____

_____

_____

    C. What kept you from accomplishing your task or delayed your progress?

_____

_____

_____

    D. What could you have done to avoid the blocker(s)? What were your options for correcting the blocker(s)?

_____

_____

_____

    E. Are you likely to encounter this type of blocker again?

_____

_____

       If so, what are you going to do about it?

_____

_____

_____

_____

Event 3

    A. Identify the event in four to ten words.

_____

_____

_____

    B. Describe the circumstances in one paragraph.

_____

_____

_____

_____

    C. What kept you from accomplishing your task or delayed your progress?

_____

_____

_____

_____

    D. What could you have done to avoid the blocker(s)? What were your options for correcting the blocker(s)?

_____

_____

_____

_____

    E. Are you likely to encounter this type of blocker again?

_____

_____

If so, what are you going to do about it?

_____

_____

_____

_____

#20

Don't assume that you know what others think or believe.

Purpose: To ensure that important information is not left to chance and to avoid misunderstanding.

"I know for a fact." "You know." "I know what you are thinking." The list goes on. People often assume that they know what others think or believe. This is a convenient but very dangerous practice.

It would be more accurate and much safer to assume that you don't "know" people, even those who are very close to you. Ask them to tell you what they mean, how they feel, or what their intentions are. Then listen very closely to what they say. Avoid reading your own agenda into their message.

To assume that you know what someone else thinks, feels, or intends invites misunderstanding. In how many of the previous activities in this book did you draw conclusions about yourself, act on them, and then reach an entirely different conclusion? In those cases, you could say that you made a mistake even with yourself. Think, then, how easily you can draw the wrong conclusion of others. The only things that you can really know about others is what they tell you—and even those things may not be accurate.

ACTIVITY

#21

Seek continuous individual development and improvement.

Purpose: To develop a habit of systematic self-improvement to avoid becoming stagnant.

I t is often difficult for people to admit that they need to continue to develop and improve—not only their knowledge but also their skills. In fact, if there were no pressures to train to keep a job or to be promoted, how many people would actively seek developmental experiences?

The fact is that learning and development are lifelong pursuits. Much of the literature written about employment, careers, and the economy points out the need for people to be in a constant learning mode.

This is your challenge for this activity: Develop a perpetual learning mode. Although a good deal of learning occurs in the classroom, learning doesn't have to be accomplished in so formal a setting. Work on improving your skills each day by simply practicing them. Find ways to expand the knowledge you have acquired on a particular subject.

Start by developing a list of skills, knowledge, and abilities you want or need to develop. For example, consider where you wish to be in a year. Then, determine what it will take to get you there. List the skills you will need to develop. Set specific deadlines for acquiring those skills. If necessary, list the subskills required to build and master the total skill. Set deadlines for accomplishing those intermediate skills.

Next, determine how you will get the resources and support to accomplish the goal you have listed. Note that you must determine *how* to get the support, not *whether* you can get the support.

Use the practice to build your schedule.

Practice

DEVELOPMENT AND IMPROVEMENT PLAN

Item	Developmental Task	Complete Date	Person Responsible	Remarks
1.				
2.				
3.				
4.				
5.				
6.				
7.				
8.				
9.				
10.				

#22

Coach subordinates.

Purpose: To share knowledge or skills with others and to develop interpersonal skills as you do so.

We are all teachers. We are all learners. There is something that each of us can learn from another. However, there are also many things that others can learn from us.

You are a reservoir of information. Some of the knowledge, skills, and abilities that you have developed through the activities in this book are examples of that. Sharing this information with others who could benefit from it will make you a valuable resource to those people.

Coaching, however, is a little different from sharing knowledge or teaching. Coaching is enabling. It is *facilitating* someone else's ability to acquire and use knowledge or a skill. It is being patient and tolerant as that person develops his or her ability. It is talking the person through a problem or a task and offering encouragement. It is sticking with a person until he or she no longer needs a coach.

Think about a person you could share your knowledge and skills with—a colleague, a neighbor, a family member, a student. All that is required, initially, is that you know something that would be useful to someone else.

Identifying what you will share and who you will share it with, however, is just a start. It is important that you develop coaching skills too. These are interpersonal skills. They will help you to provide the information in a way that facilitates your success.

#23

Make sure that you receive recognition for what you do well. Don't let anyone take away your pride.

Purpose: To ensure that you are not swayed by the negative opinions of others.

I t is often very hard to get credit and recognition for what you do—whether at work or at home. Regardless of the good that you do, others often find something to criticize. Think about that for a minute. It's a habit that seems to be ingrained in our culture. People overlook things that others do well (or just skim over them) and find the most minute excuses to criticize.

You do, however, do many things each day that are good and valuable to your organization and to your family and friends. The purpose of identifying the good and valuable things that you do is to allow yourself, indeed to force yourself, to know how you contribute to the different organizations you're a part of. Then when others concentrate only on what you *haven't* done, you can strongly, but gently, help them to see the contributions that you are making.

The start and the end of this activity rest with you. First, you must recognize the good that you do. Perhaps it would be helpful to review the practice in Activity #8, in which you identified thirty of your positive characteristics. Begin to apply some of those positive characteristics to actual circumstances in your work, home, and social life. You may even find ways that you can improve on these positive characteristics. Just don't forget that these are your *positive* characteristics—and they remain so, even if you are trying to improve on them.

Next, you may want to apply Activity #7: increase and practice your repertoire of responses. When you point out to others the good that you do, ideally, they will be able to listen, to see your point of view, and to accept the fact that you are making a valuable contribution. Some people may have trouble accepting your viewpoint, at least at first, and will continue to focus on your negative characteristics. Whether they learn to see your contributions will depend largely on how you make your point to begin with.

Of course, your approach is entirely up to you. As suggested in Activity #7, develop a variety of possible responses that you can use for different situations. You will then be able to call on the response that you feel is appropriate when the situation arises. A cool, nonconfrontational approach is generally more acceptable to most people than one that is disagreeable. Regardless of whether you feel that you have cause to "tell someone off," the more gentle approach will probably bring the most positive result, in both the short and the long term. The best result would be for others to become sensitive to the value that you add to your many relationships.

Remember that *you* are the only person you have any control over. You can try very hard to get others to see you in a different way, but *you* are really the only person who can accept or reject the actions of others, including their insistence on focusing on the negative. That is to say, if you keep in mind what you do well, no one can take that from you.

#24

Commit to the success of the organization.

Purpose: To make yourself a valuable resource to the organizations you belong to.

To commit to an organization's success is to contribute to the organization's mission and goals to the best of your ability. Strive to do so for all the organizations to which you belong—work, social, volunteer, and fraternal organizations—as well as for your family.

Perhaps you think you are indicting yourself by committing to this risk—that agreeing to complete it suggests you are not already committed to the success of these organizations. But, just think about your involvement in each of these organizations. Are your activities in them limited to your defined role? Are you an employee who goes to work, does the job, collects a paycheck, and then walks away from the job until it is time to report to work again? Is that where your relationship with your employment situation ends? (That's not to suggest that you should become a workaholic who never takes a break from work.) If you are a member of a civic group, does your involvement end at showing up for meetings?

Stop to consider the mission and goals of each organization you belong to. Does your performance live up to those organizational standards? What knowledge, skills, and abilities do you possess that would enable you and your organization to reach its ends? What new knowledge, skills, and abilities can you develop in the next twelve months that could help you contribute to the mission and goals of each of your organizations?

Decide which tasks you will be able to accomplish in the next twelve months. Be specific. Then schedule time to accomplish the tasks. Think about new ways to contribute. Commit to each and every one of your organizations. Use the practice to identify and schedule the tasks you will commit to.

Practice

1. Make a list of all the organizations you belong to.

   A. _____

   B. _____

   C. _____

   D. _____

   E. _____

   F. _____

   G. _____

   H. _____

   I. _____

   J. _____

2. Select one of these organizations, write it on the line below, and answer the remaining questions.

   _____

3. What is the mission of the organization?

_____

_____

_____

4. What are the goals of the organization?

_____

_____

_____

5. What knowledge, skills, and abilities do you currently possess that could help the organization reach its goals?

   A. _____

   B. _____

   C. _____

   D. _____

   E. _____

6. What new knowledge, skills, and abilities can you develop in the next twelve months to support the organization in reaching its ends?

   A. _____

   B. _____

   C. _____

   D. _____

   E. _____

7. Select one of the skills or abilities you listed. Schedule the time and resources to carry it out to support your organization.

_____

_____

_____

#25

Learn to communicate effectively and honestly.

Purpose: To develop tools and techniques to effectively understand others and to be understood.

All relationships depend in large part on the quality of the communication among those involved in the relationship. Yet communicating effectively is a problem in many relationships. It is truly the unique and fortunate person who doesn't have any communication problems.

Keep in mind that communicating involves more than just words. It also involves the meaning behind the words—facial expression, other body language, or even what isn't said. To communicate effectively, then, you must look beyond what others say and begin to understand what they *mean* by what they say and do. It is equally as important to ensure that others understand what your words and actions mean.

Start by striking a quick, verbal contract with those you communicate with most often. Agree that all parties will be honest and try to understand each other. Carry out this pledge in all your communications—in face-to-face dialogue, letters, memos, and reports. Don't overlook the opportunity to communicate via electronic mail and bulletin boards either.

When communicating, determine as clearly as possible the message the other person is trying to convey. To ensure that you received the right message, restate what you perceived the message to be. For example, "What I think you are saying is . . . Am I understanding what you mean?" Repeating the message will give the other party an opportunity to correct any misconceptions.

Incorporating this technique into your conversations may make them longer. But remember that this is a function of better communication. Take time to ensure that you understand and that you are understood.

*****

Perhaps by now you've tried some of the activities in this book. If this is true, then good for you. If you've chosen to read the entire chapter before attempting any of the activities, that's all right too. But the bottom line is that in order to achieve any of the rewards of the risk-taking activities, you must *do* them. Reading and learning about taking risks will, among other things, develop your confidence and expand your comfort zone. You will "get ready to" take the first step, but eventually you must actually take it.

If you haven't attempted all twenty-five activities, you may want to consider doing all of them before you go on to the next section of the book. It is not necessary, but you will be much better prepared to handle the rigors of the harder risks in the next chapter.

By now, you should realize that the real risk in this chapter has been the risk of change. Much of what you really had to risk was doing something different than you have been accustomed to. Although you stood to lose little, the potential payoffs were tremendous. Isn't that the best risk situation?

PART THREE

The High Risks— Experiencing Success Through New Ventures

In this section, you move from low- to high-risk activities. And, to use the vernacular, the "highs" will give you "highs"— those emotional peaks that evolve from executing ideas you *knew* would work, the highs resulting from experiencing success with brand-new ventures.

If you have completed most of the activities and practices in the first section, your confidence level is no doubt higher than it was before you began reading this book. Your world-radius is larger, for you have met more people, had more experiences, and expanded your responsibilities and knowledge base. You are now in a much better position to work on higher-risk activities.

The world-famous boxing coach Cus D'Amato once observed that heroes and cowards are alike in the way they experience fear. They feel the same fear, he asserted. The difference, though, is that heroes just react to fear differently. These high-risk activities will not call forth your hero traits. You will need only a modicum of courage to engage in them. But—do not think about taking the easy way out. You have come this far; you can continue. Yes, you will probably experience the stirrings of fear, or at least a distinct uneasiness with some of these activities.

If you feel they exceed the boundaries of your abilities at this time, don't do them! But if you are reasonably certain you can handle the discomfort for a short time and if you are willing to take the risk so you can profit from the experience, go for it.

You have lived with yourself for decades now, and no one knows you as you know you. If you think you can control the fear (more likely a slight tension), if you think you will feel the heady rush of daring and not the paralyzing freeze of fear, make the leap. Unlike real-life leaps, the leaps encouraged in this section can be stopped before you hit the ground. Should you not like or feel comfortable with the direction your risk activity is taking you, you can always make an adjustment in order to have a "safe landing."

Just remember the caveat that has been stressed from the very beginning—never invest more emotion, time, money, or any other resource than you can comfortably afford to lose should the risk yield less than you anticipate.

Playing it safe will seldom create the richness dreams are made of. Study the biographies of those who have "made it big"—whatever their "it" is. You will see they have been driven by their dreams; they have refused to let the boundaries of one time in their life remain as boundaries for the rest of their lives. As the Reverend Jesse Jackson states, "I was born in the slums, but the slums were not born in me!"

In a similar vein, Nancy Lee Kline, a senior secretary in a major aerospace firm, describes her refusal to let existing knowledge remain a constant. She had to learn to use a computer and become familiar with various programs, even though she felt at times that her brain was "on overload."

"I've allowed myself to look at the fear," she reveals. "Once it is brought into the light, I have found it is not as scary as it had been in my head." She explains that after she finally learned one program, the company decided to replace it with another. She recalls: "Even though I believed that I couldn't possibly learn another program, I did learn it. I have even learned to love it!"

Here's a salute to employees like Nancy Lee Kline—to people like you—who are determined to take risks and grow. The high-risk activities that follow will help fuel your determination.

#26

Keep your experimental field wide.

Purpose: To acquire new insights by combining skills from different areas of expertise.

R isk-takers are, invariably, generators of new ideas, and new ideas often come through cross-pollinating, or letting the information from one field filter into another. Ralph Waldo Emerson said that the poet is the lightning rod between the heavens and the earth. In fact, if you are willing to make such an "electric" connection, you must be able to connect the ideas from one area to the ideas of another. You must combine the forces of the "heavens" and "earth" of your own realm.

History is replete with such cross-field connections. Sewing and surgery together yielded the "zippered stitch," which allows surgeons access to an incision site merely by unzipping a temporarily implanted device, thereby eliminating the need for new incisions. Burdocks in a field and the need for easy-to-use fasteners gave us, of course, Velcro. White paint and a need to cover up typographical errors led to the office *sine qua non*—the little bottles of liquid correction fluid that no office is without.

In the corporate world, risk-takers must guard against tunnel-vision, a perspective so narrow that life itself becomes dangerously constricted. Don't lose sight of the reality that if you wish to effect change in your world of work, you must ensure that your experience is not limited only to work.

Make a practice of discussing, thinking about, and applying your outside interests to your job. Keep abreast of developments in fields other than your own. Aside from keeping your mind sharp and your focus wide, you will be constructing an intellectual springboard from which you can take creative leaps.

With such practice, the only risk you will be taking and the only investment you will be making is one of time. Take the time not only to fill out the practice questions on the next page but also to continue learning and relating the facts of one field to the facts of another.

1. Describe one of your outside interests.

_____

_____

_____

_____

_____

_____

_____

2. List ten interesting facts about that hobby or intellectual pursuit.

_____

_____

_____

_____

_____

_____

_____

_____

3. Be mentally playful: try to think of a way you could apply
   one of the above facts to the work you do.

_____

_____

_____

_____

_____

_____

_____

_____

Make a proposal.

Purpose: To gain visibility and to have your ideas recognized.

I f you came up with an especially good idea as you worked through Activity #26, a thought about how to improve some aspect of your job, for example, take that idea and fashion it into a proposal to submit to your supervisor. Don't limit yourself, of course, to the ideas you had as you worked to unleash work-related creativity in Activity #26.

Generally speaking, supervisors appreciate employees who seek to optimize corporate investments of time and money. Before submitting your idea, make sure it is well researched. Do your homework. Have data ready to persuade your supervisor that your idea really is an improvement over the way the work is currently being done. Check with individuals in other companies, if you can—with people who are in a position similar to your supervisor's. Because these people probably have a better grasp than you do of "the big picture," they can advise you about the practicality of your idea and of the likelihood that it will be accepted.

If you really believe in your idea and really would like to see it become an organizational reality, do all you can to persuade your supervisor. Here are some tips:

- Make your presentation (written or oral) as professional as possible.

- Be sure that your data are correct and convincing.

- Seek input from others you respect before you submit the proposal to your supervisor.

- Request permission to implement the idea on a pilot-project basis.

- Keep good records. Begin collecting data before your idea is implemented. Then collect data after the idea is in place. A comparison of these two sets of data will tell your supervisor how effective your idea really was.

- After the trial implementation, make another presentation to the decision-maker(s), offering irrefutable proof that your idea works!

Develop a "what-if" perspective.

Purpose: To find ways to improve existing organizational practices.

One way to build your risk-taking willingness is to loosen any "petrified" perspectives you may have. These "written-in-stone" ways of looking at the world often prevent people from finding new solutions. Often, people accept a situation, policy, or procedure simply because it exists (and has existed for as long as anyone can remember).

Instead of accepting the narrow point of view, try working from the "what-if" angle. Apply the question to any stage of production, to any level of the organization, to any aspect of your work. This perspective will allow you to stay flexible and will encourage you to try fresh and innovative approaches.

When management guru Tom Peters exhorts:

> "If you have gone a whole week without being disobedient, you are doing yourself and your organization a disservice!"

he is not advising civil disobedience or insubordination. Rather, he is fostering a questioning attitude; he is encouraging people to ask why things are done the way they are done.

The "what-if" attitude allows you to remember that the only constant is change and that everything started from zero at some point. This attitude advances your thinking, develops your creativity, and creates a climate conducive to innovation.

DON'T accept the "It's-always-been-done-this-way" attitude.

DO look for opportunities to approach work from a "what-if" framework.

Practice

Write down some of the "givens" within your organization—some of the practices, procedures, philosophical viewpoints, or long-accepted aspects of the corporate culture. For example, in many places, STAFF MEETINGS ARE HELD ON FRIDAY MORNINGS. Or, consider the widely held belief that YOU MUST HAVE AN MBA DEGREE TO MOVE INTO A MANAGEMENT POSITION. What are some traditional ways of thinking and acting in your firm?

1. _____
2. _____
3. _____
4. _____
5. _____
6. _____
7. _____
8. _____
9. _____
10. _____

Now select any one of the traditions you listed above (or all the above) and begin to explore what it would be like if the "historically correct" patterns could be altered. How would employees, and the organization itself, profit? If you uncover the kernel of a truly profitable change, develop it further. It may be risky to explore uncharted territory, but pilgrims and pioneers and outerspace peregrinators are what America is all about.

Ask for feedback.

Purpose: To narrow the gap between how others perceive you and how you perceive yourself.

Do others see you as you see yourself? There is only one way to find out: Ask! You may not like what you hear, but you can never be better than you are if you never allow a foreign thought to intrude upon your psychological shores. In many Quality-driven organizations, supervisors are now asking employees to appraise their performance as supervisors. Revolutionary, you say? Well, in many ways the Quality movement *is* revolutionary, for it encourages new ways of thinking. It encourages people to shift their paradigms, their long-held views of the world.

It is indeed risky for a supervisor to ask employees for an appraisal. But if organizations truly intend to bring greater efficiency to the workplace, or hope to improve morale and communications, then management must identify any barriers that may be standing in the way. The supervisor is putting his or her self-confidence on the line by asking such questions of employees, to be sure. But, in the long run, the investment is worth making. Open communications such as these, conducted in a professional manner, inevitably lead to win-win consequences.

It is easier, of course, to delude yourself into thinking you are perfect. You can maintain that illusion if you never allow a contrary thought to penetrate your self-applied suit of personality armor. We hide inside such suits to maintain our distance from the world. The truth is, though, that the perfect person does not exist. Life is a continuum and perfection is the absolute, the ultimate, the end of the scale. Each person falls somewhere along that continuum. Ideally, every day you will inch closer toward the "perfection" end rather than toward the end of "total flaws."

You cannot move toward the ideal, however, unless you have some input, some feedback to suggest ways that you can improve. If you find life exhilarating, you will advance from your current point on the continuum to the next milestone. To do otherwise is to stagnate. And promotions seldom come to those who stagnate.

Practice

This practice works only if you truly pay attention to what you learn from it. When you obtain feedback from others, you can either ignore that feedback and remain who you are and where you are or decide there is some merit in what you have learned. Risk-takers follow the latter course of action. They set goals to strengthen the weaknesses others perceive in them. They progress to the next point on their personal continuum.

As you look over the list of personality traits on the next page, put a check mark in front of ten—and only ten—that you feel best describe your workplace persona. But first, make a few copies of the list so that you can ask others—your supervisor, co-workers, family members, and friends—to assess you too.

If their feedback parallels your perception of yourself, then you need only think about how to achieve some of the positive qualities that you do not yet possess. But if their feedback is not entirely the same, stop to think about why people view you differently from the way you view yourself. Is there any value in being perceived the same way by everyone, including yourself? Or is it a benefit that people have widely divergent views of you?

Consider why the discrepancies exist. Share your thoughts with those you trust to give you honest but constructive feedback. You will be putting your ego on the line, but you will be getting back more than you have invested: you will be gaining self-knowledge!

Place an "X" next to ten traits that you feel describe you best.

__ active	__ impish	__ selfish
__ ambitious	__ industrious	__ sensible
__ articulate	__ inspiring	__ submissive
__ assertive	__ intelligent	__ settled
__ balanced	__ intuitive	__ tactful
__ committed	__ kind	__ tense
__ communicative	__ knowledgeable	__ technical
__ creative	__ logical	__ team-oriented
__ dependable	__ mean	__ temperate
__ dedicated	__ misinformed	__ tenacious
__ decent	__ motivated	__ tentative
__ decisive	__ nervous	__ territorial
__ diligent	__ normal	__ theoretical
__ dynamic	__ patient	__ tired
__ energetic	__ popular	__ thoughtful
__ eager	__ productive	__ ultraconservative
__ enthusiastic	__ prosaic	__ vague
__ entrepreneurial	__ professional	__ vain
__ experienced	__ pushy	__ vehement
__ flexible	__ quick	__ vindictive
__ friendly	__ sensitive	__ visual
__ funny	__ scrupulous	__ vocal
__ goal-oriented	__ selective	__ wandering
__ helpful	__ self-assured	__ warm
__ honest	__ secretive	__ petulant
__ idle	__ self-centered	__ well-read
__ impatient	__ self-indulgent	__ whining

#30

Develop a "risk retinue."

Purpose: To gain the support of others for your risk-taking efforts.

You will find that developing your risk-taking skills is easier if you have a network of supporters, a "risk retinue," if you will. "We" is always stronger than "I." If you are self-absorbed to the point of focusing only on your own efforts, you will deny yourself the synergy that comes from working with a group toward a common goal. The goal of your risk retinue should be to support you in your attempts to do something different in order to add value to your current circumstances. Even better, the members of your risk retinue might focus on helping one another, in addition to helping only you.

But whether your risk retinue concentrates only on your development or on the risk development of the group, this support base will help you avoid overlooking relevant information and will help you take advantage of latent opportunities.

To develop your risk retinue, follow these three steps:

1. List five people inside your organization who you believe will support you in your risk-taking endeavors.

   _____

   _____

   _____

   _____

   _____

2. Contact these people and ask whether they would assist you or be part of a risk-retinue group that assists members in taking measured risks.

3. Set up an informal, but definite, schedule to periodically exchange feedback and discuss plans.

#31

Develop another area of expertise.

Purpose: To add a new dimension to your working knowledge.

Your risk-taking confidence will expand if you can begin to develop some expertise in a field other than the one you are trained for. In all likelihood, the skills, knowledge, and competencies that are serving you well today will be inadequate for the future.

If you doubt the fact that your current skills may or may not be needed tomorrow, think about the number of professionals you know who have had trouble learning to use the computer. By comparison, think about students in schools today—even at the elementary level—whose capability and comfort with the computer leave many adults envious.

Of course, there is a risk in expanding your working knowledge: you might select an area of expertise that will not be utilized or valued in the future. But what will you have lost? Only the time you spent acquiring the knowledge. And how could knowledge in any form ever be considered a waste? The return on your investment includes increased intelligence, preparation for the future, greater self-confidence, and development of your leadership potential.

Here are several questions that will help you select the area in which to develop your new expertise. (You might consider discussing these questions with your supervisor as well.)

1. What skills/knowledge were most valuable in my job five years ago?

2. What skills/knowledge are most valuable in my job today?

3. What skills/knowledge will be most valuable in my job in five years?

4. What skills/knowledge do I need for my next promotion?

5. In what new direction(s) might my firm be heading?

6. If my prediction is correct, what kinds of knowledge would be valuable to have as the firm changes direction?

7. In what area does my corporate "hero" or "heroine" excel?

Create a crisis.

*Purpose: To challenge
yourself to greater heights.*

R isk-taking often includes thinking that is leading edge—or
actions that may seem curious to others who do not understand the need to develop confidence by "rezoning" their comfort
areas. Sometimes people can actually create chaos that brings out the
best in them, a deliberately imposed crisis that helps raise the meta-
phorical "bar" that separates the mediocre from the excellent.

Try moving up a deadline for a big project, for example. Rather than
finishing it by the end of next month, strive to complete it by the end
of this month. Can you do it?

The challenging deadline will stimulate you. It will focus your ener-
gies and make you conscious of potential time-wasters. Consider the
benefits: you'll have extra time to revise and polish the project, resulting in higher-quality output.

List some of the current constraints in your life—deadlines, budgets, limited resources. Then in the adjoining column, create a crisis by imposing an even more stringent constraint. Record constraints, though, that are relevant to your *professional* life.

CURRENT CONSTRAINT   **CRISIS MODE**

- Working on a project budget of $500
-
-
-
-
-
-
-
-
-

- Working on a project budget of $400
-
-
-
-
-
-
-
-
-

Be certain to build in a safety net and, if necessary, discuss your crisis-mode plan with your supervisor. Explain that by operating in this mode from time to time, you will learn more about your peak-performance levels. You can become a Roger Bannister in the corporate race for efficiency and quality. (Bannister was the first person to run a four-minute mile.)

#33

Plan a "show-and-tell" day.

Purpose: To encourage others to continue their efforts to bring about change.

Total Quality Management guru Philip Crosby advocates "show-and-tell" days to celebrate accomplishments. Consider investing some time in planning a special occasion to let others know what your team, department, or employee group has accomplished lately.

Of course, you will have to work a little harder or longer than you usually do. And, you run the risk that some people will not appreciate your efforts. But think about the potential payoff. By expending time and creative thought, you will be able to:

• Recognize the hard work of a group.

• Earn upper management's recognition of your leadership potential.

• Foster a cohesive feeling—esprit de corps, if you will—that employees feel when others take note of their work.

• Share information about what is happening in the organization.

- Create a willingness to accomplish even more, to take on more challenges.

- Increase pride in performance.

- Inspire other groups to celebrate success in a similar fashion.

The occasion can be as simple as a potluck lunch that commences with the supervisor saying a few words about the group's undertaking. Or, it can be an article in the local newspaper or a mini-conference to which interested individuals outside the firm are invited.

#34

Ask for a new assignment.

Purpose: To demonstrate your willingness to try and your ability to execute new tasks.

R isk-takers are not content to hide their light under a bushel. They are "bushel-pushers," so to speak. Sometimes—when they are at the low-risk stage of their career-enhancement program—they merely peep out from under the bushel. Later, risk-takers fling aside the bushel and let the world know what they are capable of accomplishing.

Naturally, the more publicly you announce your intention, the more widespread will be the news of your success . . . and of your failure. But risk-takers expect the former; otherwise, they would never venture into new territory. Even if their plans do not work out as anticipated, risk-takers have prepared for failure and are ready to minimize the impact.

For this activity, think of something that is not currently part of your job description but something that you would like to try doing. Select a one-time project or an activity that you would like to see incorporated into your job duties on a regular basis. Think about some of your supervisor's job duties—is there one that you feel capable of doing? Look around at others in the organization. Is someone doing something that seems especially interesting or challenging to you? Is there a project you would like to work on? Is there an upcoming organizational focus or direction you would like to learn more about?

Select such an assignment, fill out the practice worksheet on the next page, and then meet with your supervisor to discuss the new responsibility you would like to try.

Practice

1. What is the new assignment you would like to have?

   _____

   _____

2. What are some objections your supervisor might raise if you were to take on this new task?

   _____

   _____

   _____

3. What convincing rationale could you use to overcome each of your supervisor's possible objections?

   _____

   _____

   _____

4. How would the organization benefit if you took on this new assignment?

   _____

   _____

   _____

5. How will you find time to work on the new project?

   A. If necessary, which of your current   _____
      tasks could be eliminated, delegated,   _____
      or reduced in complexity?   _____

   B. Do you do some things   _____
      that do not really need   _____
      to be done?   _____

   C. Would you be willing to put in   _____
      extra time (perhaps without pay) _____
      to accomplish the new task?   _____

ACTIVITY

#35

Assess your risk-readiness.

Purpose: To assess your current state of risk-willingness.

Abraham Lincoln once commented, "I do not think much of a man who is not wiser today than he was yesterday." His indirect and early endorsement of the concept of continuous improvement is the focus of this activity. How can you better your circumstances if you do not stop occasionally to assess what they are? How can you gain more than you have if you don't take the time to gauge what you possess?

DIRECTIONS: Circle the answer that best reflects your attitude or behavior.

A. As far as change is concerned, I
   1. Fear it.
   2. Agree to it but usually experience some tension, especially at first.
   3. Create it if it does not come my way.

B. I regard myself as someone who
   1. Avoids risk.
   2. Usually "goes for the gold."
   3. Takes calculated risks.

C. When undertaking a new venture, I
   1. Act on impulse, trusting my intuition and the positive aspect of spontaneity.
   2. Engage in serious research to see what others have done in similar cases.
   3. Set up checkpoints to ensure I am on the right track.

D. I typically turn to others in my work environment
   1. When I run into a problem.
   2. At every turn because I prefer working in a team situation.
   3. Who are knowledgeable about the various stages of the project.

E. Risk-analysis means
   1. Deciding whether I can afford the time needed to engage in the risk.
   2. Consulting with others to determine the likelihood of success.
   3. Measuring the impact of potential failure.

F. As I look back over my career, I see that I have
   1. Not made as much progress as I think I could have.
   2. Advanced as a result of good fortune and the fact that people like me.
   3. Had a specific plan to be at certain points at specific times.

G. In terms of "bets,"
   1. I have an unshakable faith that life/the firm will be good to me.
   2. I bet on others to come through—and they usually do.
   3. I tend to bet on myself since I know myself best.

H. The greater the control you have, the more likely you are to influence the outcome of a situation, thus minimizing the risk involved. Betty Lehan Harragan has observed that a person's control of situations depends on that person's control of the communication system. If she is correct, you can minimize the risk of a venture by controlling it through the communication system. To what extent do you exert control over the communication system in your work environment?
   1. I have no control at all.
   2. I have limited control.
   3. I have considerable control.

I. Competition often propels people to greater action, to doing more than they thought they were capable of doing, to take risks that involve moving beyond the familiar to the unknown. What are your views of competition?
   1. It paralyzes me, creating a state of inaction.
   2. It stimulates me, moving me to action.
   3. It forces me to consider new possibilities.

J. As I look back over the years since I left school,
   1. I have more or less drifted to where I am today.
   2. I have taken one major risk that has paid off.
   3. I have taken numerous risks, most of which have paid off.

Now, give yourself points by adding all the numbers of the answers you selected. All 3s, for example, would give you a score of 30.

My score is _____.

Scoring Analysis:

10-15: You are in the Seldom Risks category. Most experts agree that it is difficult to advance your career or your fortunes unless you are willing to step outside the cautious, familiar, comfortable boundaries of your life and explore the uncharted waters awaiting you. Use this book to undertake new ventures. Continue working on the activities to advance to the Frequently Risks category.

15-22: You belong in the Frequently Risks category. You appear to be comfortable with change, but you may not be doing enough preparation or research before you take your risks. Yours is an adventurous spirit. Yet, you would be wise to carefully analyze your plans before you launch new projects in the future.

22-30: You deserve the label of Wise Risk-Taker. This is the ideal, of course, for it suggests that you do not merely gamble for the thrill of realizing high-risk results. Instead, you take into account both the positive and the negative consequences of the risk. You tend to evaluate the worst-possible scenario and decide whether you could live with it before proceeding with the risk. This is the ideal behavior.

ACTIVITY

#36

Interview a famous person in your field.

Purpose: To overcome the fear of meeting famous people and to learn more about your industry.

F amous people are surprisingly approachable. You may scoff at this assertion, but the only way to test its accuracy is to actually approach such a person. This activity urges you to do just that. "Approach" doesn't mean running over and asking for an autograph. Instead, contact the person via a formal, professionally written letter and request a personal or phone interview. Why would you want to run the risk that the famous person would simply hang up on you—assuming you could get through in the first place?

Your return on this small investment of time is virtually guaranteed to have positive results. Think about it. The only possible negative consequence that could occur is that the famous person declines the interview. End of story. (Perhaps not, actually. You may have planted a "seed" for the future in the person's head.) But the benefits that might accrue far outweigh this possibly negative outcome. Just consider these likely benefits:

• You will have learned more about your field, from an insider's point of view.

- You will have set up a network alliance that may serve you well.

- The published interview results will bring attention to you, advising others of your leadership qualities, your communication skills, and your willingness to reach out to people and firms that can provide operational insights for you and for your company.

- You will feel very, very good about your accomplishment.

Practice

These questions should help you decide who to interview, how to set up the interview, what questions to ask, and what to do with the information you glean.

1. Who comes to mind when you think about well-known figures in your occupational field?

_____

_____

_____

_____

2. What information would you supply in your letter requesting an interview? Consider each of the following:

- *Your background.* Condense it to two or three sentences.

_____

_____

_____

_____

_____

_____

- *Your reason or purpose for wanting an interview.* Make it persuasive; make it professional.

  _____

  _____

- *The questions you would like to ask.* Keep them open-ended. Avoid the trite. Try to elicit information that will benefit others in the field.

  _____

  _____

  _____

  _____

- *What you intend to do with the information you obtain.* Will you use it in a book you are writing, an article you will submit for the company newsletter, a training program you are conducting? Is there another reason?

  _____

  _____

Use the following space to draft your letter. Then, after it has been typed, properly proofread, and perhaps shared with others whose opinion you respect, MAIL IT!

_____

_____

_____

_____

_____

_____

_____

_____

_____

Resolve to make peace with the most difficult person in the organization.

Purpose: To enhance workplace cooperation.

E very organization has them: the curmudgeons who would rather snarl than smile, who would rather make spleenful comments than cooperate or be courteous. Why would you even consider befriending such an ill-tempered sort? Why would you risk the embarrassment of making a friendly overture and having that person insult you publicly?

Why? Because you will feel better when harmony overtakes hatred. The other person will feel better too—and the organization will gain as a result.

Try regarding your peace effort as a challenge, as a goal you are establishing for the next six months. Know that the drain on your emotions and your energy will be gone at the end of that time. Converting a normally nasty person into a cooperative working partner is not an easy task.

Think about the person who will become your mission for the next several months. Is he or she well-liked by others? If so, perhaps *you* are doing something that offends that person. Sometimes it takes very little to learn what that is and to make adjustments.

If the person is genuinely disliked by most people, then he or she is already at a disadvantage. If you, by comparison, have a number of co-worker friends, then you are already more fortunate than this person and can afford to be somewhat generous in your friendship overtures. Have you considered that this person may have problems no one knows about, problems that may be coloring his or her view of the world? Keep in mind that a person's outer behavior is often the result of an inner turmoil you may not understand.

There are, however, some truly difficult people in the world. They thrive on being difficult. No amount of persuasion will change such a person's attitude. Chances are, though, that this type of person does not work in your company. If the individual you are considering befriending falls into this category, avoid him or her. On the other hand, if the person simply does not get along well with others, make an overture to improve your working relationship.

Here are a few approaches that may work. Select the one you think would best fit your circumstances and give it a try. If it doesn't work, try a second approach a few weeks later. And then a third.

- Approach the person and simply explain that you are interested in developing good working relationships with others in the office. Delicately admit that you've not really had a chance to work with him or her closely before and would like the opportunity to develop a smoother connection from this point on.

- Find out about an interest or hobby this person has. Then, the next time you come across an article the person may be interested in, cut it out and share it. Use the article as a conversational gamut, a point of contact, a focus that will make future conversations easier.

- Ask to meet with the person. Explain that your organization's new emphasis on Total Quality Management, which encourages open communication with internal customers, has caused you to realize that the work flow is more efficient when co-workers can discuss their various needs. Ask what you might do differently to make the person's job easier.

- Be direct. Ask the person whether you've done anything in the past that has caused him or her some difficulty. Using your diplomatic skills, try to learn why a problem exists and what can be done in the future to minimize the dissension.

Here are sample statements that difficult people have been known to make. Try to come up with a diplomatic, harmonizing response.

You:	Good morning.
Curmudgeon:	What's good about it?
Your response:	_____

You:	Could you tally these figures for me?
Curmudgeon:	Do it yourself. I don't have time.
Your response:	_____

You:	That's a nice shirt you're wearing.
Curmudgeon:	Don't try to get Brownie points from me. I can't do anything to advance your career. And even if I could, I wouldn't.
Your response:	_____

You:	Here's the report you wanted.
Curmudgeon:	I'm certain it displays your usual ineptitude.
Your response:	_____

You:	I've called this meeting so we can learn more about TQM principles.
Curmudgeon:	It's another asinine administrative acronym. And it will fail like all the others.
Your response:	_____

You:	As team leader, I'd like to talk about the feasibility of meeting our target date for completion.
Curmudgeon:	Maybe if you were around more often, we'd have completed the project by now.
Your response:	_____

#38

Volunteer to train others.

Purpose: To develop your training skills and to share knowledge with others.

M anagement consultant Andrew Sherwood has listed the ability to train others as a critical skill for advancement. Based on this recommendation, try instructing a group of co-workers about a specific skill or set of ideas. You don't need to become a corporate trainer or neglect your job duties in order to put on training workshops.

Instead, just think about some phase of your job in which you are considered to be an expert. (If that label could not accurately be applied to you at this time, resolve to develop your reputation in some specific area of your profession. Then, reconsider this activity.) What is the best vehicle for sharing your expertise with others?

- Presenting a brief report at a staff meeting

- Incorporating your information into the orientation program

- Putting on a full-day program

- Making a delivery to upper management

- Conducting a training program in concert with the training department or the human resources department

- Conducting a special after-hours class for those interested in the topic

- Other possibilities:

  _____

  _____

  _____

  _____

As you plan your training session, keep in mind the following points:

- What is my purpose?

- How can I keep the interest of my audience?

- What is the most important information I need to share?

- How can I show them that this information is relevant to their jobs?

- What questions are they likely to ask?

#39

Form a team. Ask to be the team leader.

Purpose: To gain leadership experience.

A s the team succeeds, so do its members. As the team fails, so do its members—especially its leader. And therein lies the risk: although team members share equally in the success and failure of their efforts, the team leader carries a special responsibility. But, as a team leader, if your preparation is careful, if you have a worthwhile project, if you are able to energize your team, and if you can persuade upper management of the merit of your plan, you are in a unique position to effect change and, thus, see the greatest possible return on your investment of time and, perhaps, ego.

Choose a project that you would like to direct. To begin, brainstorm some areas of your workplace that could be made more efficient. What procedures are taking too long? Or have unnecessary steps built in? What processes involve duplicated efforts? Also contemplate things your department is not currently doing that you think it should be doing. Or, deliberate about the things you do but don't do as well as you could.

In the space below, list fifteen ideas that could become projects for improvement.

1. _____
2. _____
3. _____
4. _____
5. _____
6. _____
7. _____
8. _____
9. _____
10. _____
11. _____
12. _____
13. _____
14. _____
15. _____

Now select one of the ideas above and invite others to work with you as a team to improve the current situation.

ACTIVITY

#40

Go on interviews, even if you are not ready, willing, or able to leave your current job.

Purpose: To acquire familiarity with the interview process and to sharpen your interview skills.

A s always, when you ponder the consequence of a risk, you think about what you have to lose versus what you stand to gain. With this activity, you are urged to go on promotional informational interviews—either inside or outside your company.

Here's what you might lose:

• Your supervisor's confidence in you. He or she might learn that you are setting up interviews and mistakenly believe that you are ready to quit your job. To circumvent this possibility, you can explain in advance that you are going on such interviews simply to gain experience and to learn the value of your talents to comparable firms. (Sometimes the fact that an employee is "shopping around" is sufficient stimulus for management to realize how valuable the employee really is. Some employees who have gone on informational interviews have even been given a pay raise. No company wants to lose valuable, valued employees.)

• Your time. You might need to take some time off work.

Here's what you might gain:

• Knowledge of just how marketable you really are

• Information about a "dream job" opportunity that you are qualified for

• Interview skills

• Networking contacts

• Further information about your industry or field

• Greater self-confidence

• The chance to let others know who you are and what you plan for the future

Ask your supervisor to help you plan your career path.

Purpose: To obtain a management perspective on the likelihood of attaining your career goals.

You can be assured that you will need more than your daily dose of self-confidence to tackle this activity. That's because you don't ask your supervisor for this kind of assistance on a daily basis. What's the risk factor here?

Your supervisor may reply that he or she is too busy to assist you. Or, you may hear something that you weren't expecting—that your future looks dim. Your supervisor may feel threatened, thinking that you are out to take over his or her job or that you are more interested in promotion than loyalty to the firm. But these "perhaps" possibilities recede into the background when they are juxtaposed with the advantages you will derive from this career strategy. Consider these:

• If your supervisor truly feels you have no future beyond your current position, wouldn't you rather know it now than five years from now?

- If your supervisor is unwilling to serve as your official or unofficial mentor, you will be able to find someone else to help you.

- If the supervisor agrees to prime you for promotion, you will have an experienced guide advising you as you make decisions and solve problems.

- You will be saving time, effort, and energy by making the right moves, using the proper rungs to hoist you as you ascend the corporate ladder.

- Your self-confidence will increase as you work more closely with a supervisor who has demonstrated faith in your abilities by virtue of his or her willingness to serve as your career advisor.

Practice

Circle the statement you feel would work best when you approach your supervisor about career planning. Discuss your selections with a co-worker or friend. There are no "right" answers. You and you alone are the best judge of the circumstances, the personalities, the timing, and the corporate mind-set.

1. **Requesting the appointment**
   - Bob, do you have a few minutes?
   - I'd like to make an appointment to meet with you soon about my career.
   - I need your help, Mr. Forest. Could I stop by after work today?

2. **Explaining your intent**

   - This will only take a few minutes. I'm wondering what you think I should do to improve my chances for promotion.

   - I have some definite career goals in mind. I'd like to go over them with you and get your input on them.

   - In many ways, you are a role model for me. I'd like to do what you have done in this company and hope I can count on your support.

3. **Specifying the extent of your supervisor's involvement**

   - I would like to meet with you periodically to review my progress.

   - I hope we can keep this informal. As the need arises, would you be willing to sit down with me and give me the benefit of your advice?

   - I'd like to check with you prior to making any major moves or decisions.

4. **Summarizing the meeting**

   - You understand, then, that within five years, I would like to be at this level in the organization. And you agree that you will keep me informed of the opportunities and leads I should pursue.

   - We'll meet, then, on the first Monday of every month for an update.

   - I'm asking only that you direct me to situations that would increase my likelihood of being promoted to supervisor within two years.

5. **Concluding the meeting**

   - Thanks so much, Bob.

   - Please tell me how I can repay your kindness.

   - I'll do all I can to see that your faith in me is justified.

ACTIVITY

#42

Prepare a "success analysis."

Purpose: To determine your probability of success with a major risk-taking endeavor.

We take some risks without deliberation. They are almost intuitive reactions to circumstances. Deciding whether we can make it through an intersection before the light turns red, for example, does not require much planning. Other risks, by comparison, deserve careful forethought and thorough investigation.

Use the space below to record some major risks you have thought about taking—switching careers, seeking a new position, starting your own company, deciding to go for a promotion, and so on. What changes would you like to pursue in the workplace or in your life in general?

_____

_____

_____

_____

_____

_____

_____

Next, perform a success analysis. The success analysis is actually an equation consisting of four factors:

- *History:* What is the precedent for this sort of endeavor?

- *Practicality:* How likely is my plan to work?

- *Skill Fit:* How prepared or capable am I in this regard?

- *Resources:* Realistically, what resources do I have to carry this out?

Each of the factors is given a rating, or valence, on a 4-point scale. (See the chart in the practice.) The total of the four valences is then divided by 4. The closer the resulting number is to 4, the greater your likelihood of success with a particular venture.

Practice

What is the risk or new project you are contemplating?

_____

Next, determine your likelihood for success with this project by rating each factor according to the following chart. Write the valence number next to each factor.

History _____   **Practicality** _____   **Skill Fit** _____   **Resources** _____

Valence

1. This has never been done.	This probably would not work.	I don't know anything about it.	I have neither the time nor the money to pursue it.
2. This has been tried, but not successfully.	It just might work here.	I know a little about this.	I could probably make time for it.
3. People are not very interested in this.	I believe we have what we need to make it work.	I have some knowledge and experience with things like this.	I could probably get management support.
4. We have a precedent for similar success.	This is doable, and in the near future.	I am confident I can make this work.	We have everything we need; it'll work.

Now, transfer your rating for each factor to the appropriate blank in the success formula below.

Success Likelihood
(H_____ + P_____ + SF_____ + R_____) = _____ ≠ 4 = _____

The higher your final number is to 4 (obtained by adding your four valence numbers and then dividing by four), the greater the likelihood that your project will be successful.

#43

Ask the "second-mortgage" question.

Purpose: To gauge the extent of your faith in a risk you are considering.

In his widely acclaimed book *Intrapreneuring*, Gifford Pinchot III writes about a Fortune 100 president who asks, "Would you take a second mortgage on your home for this idea?" This is how the president tests the extent of employee commitment to a project. None of the activities in this book requires such a drastic test. But, the question is a good one for assessing the extent of your belief in a new undertaking.

How certain are you about the worth of the risk you are considering or proposing to others? Is your dedication to the idea so fierce that you would be willing to invest heavily to make it a success? Is your allegiance to this new concept or new philosophy so profound that you would be willing to make a "second-mortgage" statement such as "Just let me try. If it doesn't work, I will give up the next promotion, or work overtime for six months without pay, or forego the annual bonus"?

Of course, if you are confident enough to propose such a sacrifice in defense of your idea, you must offset it with a statement such as, "And if it does work, I expect an immediate career advancement or financial reward."

#44

Volunteer to do a job no one else wants to do.

Purpose: To make a contribution to the organization and to allow others to see your potential.

C onsider handling a job no one else in your organization would go near. Perhaps the reluctance of your colleagues to do this job is based on the fact that the work is unpleasant or that its failure is virtually guaranteed. Perhaps others see it as a low-visibility project, or perhaps they regard it more as charity work than as career-enhancement work.

Yet, at least once during your career, assume a project that will probably benefit others more than it will benefit you—at least it will seem that way on the surface. In reality (assuming you do a creditable job), you will be stockpiling any number of credits in your vocational ledger:

• Others will recognize that you aren't afraid of hard work or unpopular assignments and will be grateful to you.

• You will probably be helping others. There are few rewards in life quite so gratifying.

- You can cite this accomplishment later on and use it as leverage as you remind a supervisor of what you have done for the company.

Volunteer for no more than a few months—you should show your willingness to pitch in—not a willingness to be a martyr.

Consider these questions as you decide which job to volunteer for:

1. What is one job that needs to be done but no one wants to do?

   _____
   _____
   _____

2. How long would it take you to do that job and do it well?

   _____
   _____
   _____

3. How would doing it benefit others? How would it benefit you?

   _____
   _____
   _____
   _____
   _____
   _____
   _____

Think a Janusian thought; develop a bright idea; create an organizational reality.

Purpose: To gain confidence in your ability to improve a workplace situation.

L ove and marriage, as the popular song tells us, go together like a horse and carriage. So do innovation and risk. In the words of Konrad Adenauer, a former German chancellor, "We all live under the same sky, but we don't have the same horizon."

Consider stretching your horizon, to take a bright idea and make it an organizational reality, even if others, living under the same corporate sky, do not share your idea.

Begin with this creativity-enhancing exercise in the practice. It's based on the ancient Roman god Janus, after whom the month of January is named. Janus was profiled on Roman coins, facing both ways. And so the month of January both looks toward the new year and recollects the old year. Janusian thinking forces you to think of opposites and then to see how elements of one extreme might be incorporated into the essence of the other extreme to achieve a workable synthesis.

In the spaces in the far lefthand column, write down ten words, preferably nouns, associated with your job. (For the time being, ignore the words in the righthand column.)

1.	_____	_____	honor
2.	_____	_____	friend
3.	_____	_____	gossip
4.	_____	_____	future
5.	_____	_____	random-access
6.	_____	_____	quotation
7.	_____	_____	laugh
8.	_____	_____	fall
9.	_____	_____	dog
10.	_____	_____	speed

Next, in the middle column, write a word that is a polar opposite of the word in the first column. Stop and do it now. You can return to this page later for the remaining directions.

The final step is the most difficult in a sense, for it requires intellectual playfulness and most people have not taken the time to let such thinking evolve. Look now at all three words in every row. Look at them a second time, and even a third or fourth, if necessary. You may need to sleep on this strange combination of words, for it is during the incubation period (when strange combinations merge into workable forms) that innovative ideas are usually born.

For example, creative writing instructors often force students to consider the juxtaposition of words not usually related and then to fashion a story or poem around this new combination. If you always think the safe thoughts, if you never venture away from your existing knowledge, if you never read outside your field, chances are you will overlook creative sources.

You will not be able to come up with good ideas for all of these combinations but *one* of them should ignite some innovative flames. Throughout your life, continue to think Janusian thoughts; combine the old with the new, the unfamiliar with the known.

Return to the list after a day or so and try to evolve a bright idea that no one in the company has ever had or developed before. Describe your idea in the following space, telling both what it is but also what it is not.

This idea includes:

_____

_____

_____

_____

_____

_____

This idea does not include:

_____

_____

_____

_____

_____

_____

Next, select someone in the organization (it may or may not be your supervisor) who you feel would be a "champion" for this idea. Ask this person what needs to be done, what steps must be followed, what approval must be obtained in order to embed this bright idea as a permanent fixture in the corporate culture. Work closely with this person and solicit his or her support in converting this thought to reality.

ACTIVITY

#46

Find "devils" to advocate barriers.
Purpose: To examine a potential risk from every possible angle.

Q uick! What is a professional risk you have been thinking about taking for a while? Record it here:

_____

Now list the names of three people who can give you a dozen ideas why that plan won't work:

_____

_____

_____

(Most people can think of more reasons why a good idea *won't* work than reasons why it could.)

Your next step is to sit down and explore at length the objections these three people have. These people may be natural nay-sayers or doom-and-gloom types. Or they may be naturally negative individuals who tend not to dream but to puncture holes in the dreamballoons of those who dare. They may even be people who genuinely care about you and who do not want to see you waste your time or money or emotions on a scheme *they* consider too risky.

Write down all their objections and then begin to objectively assess your risk in view of these objections. Consult with others. Investigate further. If—after all your calculations—you still believe the idea merits implementation, if you honestly feel the barriers can be removed, then "go for the gold."

You may not win medals, but you will surely know the thrill of trying, of overcoming odds that may initially seem insurmountable.

Write an article.

Purpose: To share your views with others in the same field and to enhance your career.

It's been observed that every time we put words on paper, we allow others to see into our brains. Perhaps for that reason alone—the possibility that others may find our "brain-view" disorganized or sloppy or lacking profundity—many people dislike writing. And yet, writing skills appear over and over on lists of the most valuable skills employers seek in employees.

Yes, there is some risk involved in this activity, the risk that your ideas may be mocked, the risk that you may make an error in public, the risk that others may disagree with your point of view. But as you have repeatedly read in this book, the wisest risk-takers anticipate the worst but plan for the best.

Your article need not be long, but it should express an interesting point of view, one that affords a new slant or "spin" on a topic of interest to your professional colleagues. You could have the article printed in the company newsletter, but why not make a major risk investment here? (After all, you're nearly at the end of this book.) Why not try to publish your article in a reputable trade journal so that like-minded professionals throughout the nation will have a chance to respond to your ideas? Timidity and derring-doers are seldom mentioned in the same breath, as you must know by now. Think big!

Here are some recommendations for your journalistic journey:

• Check back issues of the publication to ensure that your topic is timely.

• Send a query letter to the editor.

• Assuming there is interest, use a "mindmapping" or brain-storming technique to record your initial thoughts on the subject.

• Submit your draft to an esteemed colleague.

• Edit, edit, edit.

#48

Organize a conference.

Purpose: To expand your organizational skills and to make a name for yourself.

Be forewarned: There's a lot that could go wrong if you undertake this activity. But as a risk-taker, you obviously feel there is more that could go right than wrong. You are probably wondering what theme you could plan a conference around. If you can't think of one right away, all you need to do is ask ten people for their ideas. You will probably receive twenty to thirty ideas faster than you can write them down.

You will no doubt need management approval before you begin this project. If you don't receive it, try planning a conference for an outside group such as a church or professional organization.

What do you stand to gain from your investment of time and energy? Three obvious answers come to mind: the people you will meet, the reputation you will develop, and the organizational skills you will refine. What are some other possible advantages you will realize?

_____

_____

_____

Naturally, there are some possible disadvantages as well. If there were none, this activity would not be considered a risk. Planning such a conference could physically drain you. But the good thing about such an energy expenditure is that it is finite. Once the conference is over, you can resume your normal schedule. Another possible disadvantage is that the conference may not receive rave reviews from attendees. But the non-rave reviews are the ones that will help you improve your performance. You will learn from them so that next year's conference will be even better than this year's.

Practice

The fishbone diagram (also known as the cause-and-effect diagram or the Ishikawa diagram, after the name of its originator, Kaoru Ishikawa) may help you organize your initial thoughts about the conference.

It works like this. List your ideas under each category of the fishbone. You may even wish to add other categories. Then go back and make additions or corrections to your list. Check with others to see if you have missed anything. Then begin your plans, point by point, using your fishbone as a guide.

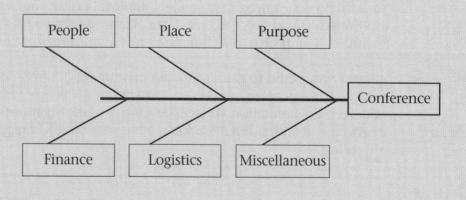

#49

Be a founder of a professional organization.

Purpose: To fulfill a professional need and to create a community of professionals with similar interests.

Too risky, you say? Who can I get to join? What if no one joins? How do we write the constitution? How big should the group be? Do we have to follow Robert's Rules of Order? What would be our purpose? When would we meet? What if we can't agree on a charter? What if they won't let me be the leader?

All of these questions and more must be wrestled with. But remember. There are precedents to direct you. Look up the history of other professional organizations. You will find that most of them started with one person's desire and the dedication of only a small group of followers. Their original charters or constitutions were usually brief documents that have been amended over time.

Your association can assume any focus or direction, but you should select a core philosophy that you are passionately committed to. Your center may be a group of other professionals with similar concerns: a group of engineers or lawyers or secretaries devoted to bettering their profession. Or it could be a group of individuals with dissimilar titles but a common interest: community advocates for Total Quality Management, for example. You may find that time-honored themes such as leadership or ethics or communications or time-management could be the basis for the formation. Or even risk-taking.

Whatever you select, you will simultaneously be selecting an opportunity to demonstrate your leadership. Who knows where that leadership and your risk-taking initiative can lead?

#50

Make a videotape or an audiocassette about your organization.

Purpose: To explore a new medium and to give your organization a historical gift.

Your first response will undoubtedly be, "But I don't know anything about making videotapes or audiocassettes!" So? Neither did those who make such tapes for a living when they first began. No one is born with these or any other skills. They acquire them through learning. Even as you read this, someone is learning how to make an audio or videotape.

How could the tapes be used? In any number of ways. In presentations for customers. As part of an orientation program. At conferences. At retirement parties. In after-hours classes. As promotions. As incentives for employees. And these are but a few ideas.

What if your firm already has such a tape? Well, they may have the videotape but probably not the audiocassette. An interesting audiocassette is something employees may wish to purchase and listen to as they drive to and from work. You might even produce a series of them. If tapes on corporate issues already exist, you could always make tapes about the professional organization you founded in Activity #49.

As far as resources are concerned, you probably have more available to you than you realize. If you work in a large organization, there is probably a cadre of audio-visual experts nearby, most of whom would probably be more than happy to help.

Even if you do not have a full department working to these ends, you probably have co-workers who are audio-video buffs and who may be willing to work with you (and share their equipment) for no fee other than the "glory" of being acknowledged in the credits. You can take courses, read books, or talk to others (in other companies or in Hollywood) who have made similar productions. The Academy Award may never be yours, but surely you deserve an award for risk-taking achievement.

PART FOUR

Reaping the Rewards—Planning Your Own Risks

Throughout this book, one thing has been made perfectly clear: risk-taking can be *foolhardy*—governed by chance and an overriding desire to gamble, or it can be *deliberate*—governed by calculation and planning. You have been given fifty activities and numerous practices to develop the kind of risk-taking that is synonymous with winning strategies: namely, the kind that depends on logical preparation for both the success and the possible failure of the endeavor.

Carrying out the activities in this book will, hopefully, have given you enough confidence and rewards to spur you on to additional risk-taking opportunities. And that—the ability to tackle your own risk situations head on—is the best reward for the time and effort you have spent working through the activities in this book.

To help you plan and organize these additional risk-taking activities, this section of the book provides several planning sheets that are similar in format to the activities you have already completed.

As you "go it alone," remember this: Risk-takers tend to be visionaries—individuals with well-delineated views of where they wish to go in life, rather than vague notions of where life will take them. Often, their vision includes others. And so, although risk-taking truly benefits the risk-taker, it typically benefits the organization as well.

Risk-takers are also adventurers: the faint-of-heart are seldom seen exercising their leadership potential. Improvement without some degree of risk is an oxymoron, a contradictory set of terms. In order to advance, you must move forward, you must leave the present comfort for the future unknown, which—at some point—will become the present comfort all over again and, therefore, ripe for change. Risk-takers do not fear change; indeed, they welcome it. They know the heady exhilaration, the undeniable emotional rush derived from executing a well-conceived plan and seeing it materialize into beneficial results.

Risk-takers are also realists. They know they cannot control every facet of life, but they build in contingency plans for those unpredictable events that threaten even the minutely programmed strategies. The ideal risk-taker does not back down in the face of adversity. More likely than not, he or she is challenged by it, energized by the thought that there may be more to give than anticipated.

Calvin Coolidge wisely observed that "No person was ever honored for what he received. Honor has been the reward for what he gave." After reading this book, you may go on to implement the ideas born of these risk-taking activities. And some of those ideas will be so good that others will have no choice but to recognize you and the contributions you have made.

If it weren't for the risk-takers and their unshakable faith in themselves and in the forces that can create a better tomorrow, most of us would not be here today. May all your risks reap the reward of improved circumstances!

ACTIVITY #1

Risk: _____
_____

Purpose: _____
_____
_____

Planned Activity _____
_____

Results _____
_____

Follow-up _____
_____

ACTIVITY #2

Risk: _____
_____

Purpose: _____
_____
_____

Planned Activity _____
_____

Results _____
_____

Follow-up _____
_____

ACTIVITY #3

Risk: _____

_____

Purpose: _____

_____

_____

Planned Activity _____

_____

Results _____

_____

Follow-up _____

_____

ACTIVITY #4

Risk: _____

_____

Purpose: _____

_____

_____

Planned Activity _____

_____

Results _____

_____

Follow-up _____

_____

ACTIVITY #5

Risk: _____
_____

Purpose: _____
_____
_____

Planned Activity _____
_____

Results _____
_____

Follow-up _____
_____

ACTIVITY #6

Risk: _____
_____

Purpose: _____
_____
_____

Planned Activity _____
_____

Results _____
_____

Follow-up _____
_____

ACTIVITY #7

Risk: _____

_____

Purpose: _____

_____

_____

Planned Activity _____

_____

Results _____

_____

Follow-up _____

_____

ACTIVITY #8

Risk: _____

_____

Purpose: _____

_____

_____

Planned Activity _____

_____

Results _____

_____

Follow-up _____

_____

ACTIVITY
#9

Risk: _____
_____

Purpose: _____
_____
_____

Planned Activity _____
_____

Results _____
_____

Follow-up _____
_____

ACTIVITY
#10

Risk: _____
_____

Purpose: _____
_____
_____

Planned Activity _____
_____

Results _____
_____

Follow-up _____
_____

ACTIVITY

#11

Risk: _____

_____

Purpose: _____

_____

_____

Planned Activity _____

_____

Results _____

_____

Follow-up _____

_____

ACTIVITY

#12

Risk: _____

_____

Purpose: _____

_____

_____

Planned Activity _____

_____

Results _____

_____

Follow-up _____

_____

Bibliography and Suggested Reading

Allison, Mary Ann and Eric W. Allison. *Managing Up, Managing Down: How to Be a Better Manager and Get What You Want from Your Boss and Your Staff.* New York: Cornerstone Library, 1984.

Avadian, Brenda. *Drive North in Your Career!* Lancaster, CA: North Star Books, 1992.

Blake, Robert and Jane S. Mouton. *The New Managerial Grid.* Houston, TX: Gulf Publishing, 1978.

Blanchard, Kenneth and Spencer Johnson. *The One Minute Manager.* New York: Berkley Books, 1983.

Bramson, Robert M. *Coping With Difficult People.* New York: Anchor Press/Doubleday, 1981.

De Pree, Max. *Leadership Is an Art.* New York: Doubleday, 1989.

Deming, W. Edwards. *Out of the Crisis.* Cambridge, MA: MIT Center for Advanced Engineering Study, 1986.

145

Drucker, Peter. *Managing in Turbulent Times*. New York: Harper & Row, 1980.

Drucker, Peter. *The Effective Executive*. New York: Harper & Row, 1985.

Dudley, Denise M. *Every Woman's Guide to Career Success*. Mission, KS: SkillPath, 1991.

Ewing, David W. *Do It My Way or You're Fired!* New York: John Wiley & Sons, 1983.

Feder, Michal E. *A Personal Guide to Managing Projects and Priorities*. Mission, KS: SkillPath, 1989.

Ferguson, Marilyn. *The Aquarian Conspiracy*. Los Angeles: J.P. Tarcher, 1980.

Foy, Nancy. *The Yin and Yang of Organizations*. New York: Morrow, 1981.

Friedman, Paul. *How to Deal With Difficult People*. Mission, KS: SkillPath, 1989.

Geneen, Harold. *Managing*. Garden City, N.Y.: Doubleday, 1984.

Grove, Andrew. *High Output Management*. New York: Random House, 1983.

Hammermesh, Richard G., ed. *Strategic Management*. New York: John Wiley & Sons, 1983.

Hiam, Alexander. *The Vest-Pocket CEO: Decision-Making Tools for Executives*. New York: Prentice Hall, 1990.

Kennedy, Allan A. and Terrance E. Deal. *Corporate Cultures: The Rites and Rituals of Corporate Life*. Reading, MA: Addison-Wesley, 1982.

Mackay, Harvey. *Beware the Naked Man Who Offers You His Shirt*. New York: Morrow, 1990.

Mali, Paul, ed. *Management Handbook: Operating Guidelines, Techniques and Practices*. New York: John Wiley & Sons, 1981.

McCaskey, Michael B. *The Executive Challenge: Managing Change and Ambiguity*. Boston: Pitman, 1982.

Naisbitt, John and Patricia Aburdene. *Re-inventing the Corporation: Transforming Your Job and Your Company for the New Information Society*. New York: Warner Books, 1985.

Ohmae, Kenichi. *The Mind of a Strategist: The Art of Japanese Management*. New York: McGraw-Hill, 1982.

Ouchi, William G. *Theory Z: How American Business Can Meet the Japanese Challenge*. Reading, MA: Addison-Wesley, 1981.

Poley, Michelle Fairfield. *A Winning Attitude: How to Develop Your Most Important Asset*. Mission, KS: SkillPath, 1992.

Sargent, Alice G. *The Androgynous Manager*. New York: AMACOM, 1981.

Temme, Jim. *Productivity Power: 250 Great Ideas for Being More Productive*. Mission, KS: SkillPath, 1993.

Torpey, William G. *Federal Management Initiatives*. Richmond, VA: Byrd Publishing, 1984.

Towers, Mark. *A Manager's Guide for Active Empowerment*. Mission, KS: SkillPath, 1993.

Available From SkillPath Publications

Self-Study Sourcebooks

Climbing the Corporate Ladder: What You Need to Know and Do to Be a Promotable Person *by Barbara Pachter and Marjorie Brody*

Coping With Supervisory Nightmares: 12 Common Nightmares of Leadership and What You Can Do About Them *by Michael and Deborah Singer Dobson*

Defeating Procrastination: 52 Fail-Safe Tips for Keeping Time on Your Side *by Marlene Caroselli, Ed.D.*

Discovering Your Purpose *by Ivy Haley*

Going for the Gold: Winning the Gold Medal for Financial Independence *by Lesley D. Bissett, CFP*

Having Something to Say When You Have to Say Something: The Art of Organizing Your Presentation *by Randy Horn*

Info-Flood: How to Swim in a Sea of Information Without Going Under *by Marlene Caroselli, Ed.D.*

The Innovative Secretary *by Marlene Caroselli, Ed.D.*

Letters & Memos: Just Like That! *by Dave Davies*

Mastering the Art of Communication: Your Keys to Developing a More Effective Personal Style *by Michelle Fairfield Poley*

Obstacle Illusions: Coverting Crisis to Opportunity *by Marlene Caroselli, Ed.D.*

Organized for Success! 95 Tips for Taking Control of Your Time, Your Space, and Your Life *by Nanci McGraw*

A Passion to Lead! How to Develop Your Natural Leadership Ability *by Michael Plumstead*

P.E.R.S.U.A.D.E.: Communication Strategies That Move People to Action *by Marlene Caroselli, Ed.D.*

Productivity Power: 250 Great Ideas for Being More Productive *by Jim Temme*

Promoting Yourself: 50 Ways to Increase Your Prestige, Power, and Paycheck *by Marlene Caroselli, Ed.D.*

Proof Positive: How to Find Errors Before They Embarrass You *by Karen L. Anderson*

Risk-Taking: 50 Ways to Turn Risks Into Rewards *by Marlene Caroselli, Ed.D. and David Harris*

Stress Control: How You Can Find Relief From Life's Daily Stress *by Steve Bell*

The Technical Writer's Guide *by Robert McGraw*

Total Quality Customer Service: How to Make It Your Way of Life *by Jim Temme*

Write It Right! A Guide for Clear and Correct Writing *by Richard Andersen and Helene Hinis*

Your Total Communication Image *by Janet Signe Olson, Ph.D.*

Handbooks

The ABC's of Empowered Teams: Building Blocks for Success *by Mark Towers*

Assert Yourself! Developing Power-Packed Communication Skills to Make Your Points Clearly, Confidently, and Persuasively *by Lisa Contini*

Breaking the Ice: How to Improve Your On-the-Spot Communication Skills *by Deborah Shouse*

The Care and Keeping of Customers: A Treasury of Facts, Tips, and Proven Techniques for Keeping Your Customers Coming BACK! *by Roy Lantz*

Challenging Change: Five Steps for Dealing With Change *by Holly DeForest and Mary Steinberg*

Dynamic Delegation: A Manager's Guide for Active Empowerment *by Mark Towers*

Every Woman's Guide to Career Success *by Denise M. Dudley*

Exploring Personality Styles: A Guide for Better Understanding Yourself and Your Colleagues *by Michael Dobson*

Grammar? No Problem! *by Dave Davies*

Great Openings and Closings: 28 Ways to Launch and Land Your Presentations With Punch, Power, and Pizazz *by Mari Pat Varga*

Hiring and Firing: What Every Manager Needs to Know *by Marlene Caroselli, Ed.D. with Laura Wyeth, Ms.Ed.*

How to Be a More Effective Group Communicator: Finding Your Role and Boosting Your Confidence in Group Situations *by Deborah Shouse*

How to Deal With Difficult People *by Paul Friedman*

Learning to Laugh at Work: The Power of Humor in the Workplace *by Robert McGraw*

Making Your Mark: How to Develop a Personal Marketing Plan for Becoming More Visible and More Appreciated at Work *by Deborah Shouse*

Meetings That Work *by Marlene Caroselli, Ed.D.*

The Mentoring Advantage: How to Help Your Career Soar to New Heights *by Pam Grout*

Minding Your Business Manners: Etiquette Tips for Presenting Yourself Professionally in Every Business Situation *by Marjorie Brody and Barbara Pachter*

Misspeller's Guide *by Joel and Ruth Schroeder*

Motivation in the Workplace: How to Motivate Workers to Peak Performance and Productivity *by Barbara Fielder*

NameTags Plus: Games You Can Play When People Don't Know What to Say *by Deborah Shouse*

Networking: How to Creatively Tap Your People Resources *by Colleen Clarke*

New & Improved! 25 Ways to Be More Creative and More Effective *by Pam Grout*

Power Write! A Practical Guide to Words That Work *by Helene Hinis*

The Power of Positivity: Eighty ways to energize your life *by Joel and Ruth Schroeder*

Putting Anger to Work For You *by Ruth and Joel Schroeder*

Reinventing Your Self: 28 Strategies for Coping With Change *by Mark Towers*

Saying "No" to Negativity: How to Manage Negativity in Yourself, Your Boss, and Your Co-Workers *by Zoie Kaye*

The Supervisor's Guide: The Everyday Guide to Coordinating People and Tasks *by Jerry Brown and Denise Dudley, Ph.D.*

Taking Charge: A Personal Guide to Managing Projects and Priorities *by Michal E. Feder*

Treasure Hunt: 10 Stepping Stones to a New and More Confident You! *by Pam Grout*

A Winning Attitude: How to Develop Your Most Important Asset! *by Michelle Fairfield Poley*

For more information, call 1-800-873-7545.

Notes

Notes

Notes